I0461621

PRAISE FOR BEYOND WORDS

For decades at MAPS, we've worked to legitimize psychedelic therapy through rigorous science. But science alone cannot address the profound spiritual openings these medicines often catalyze. *Beyond Words* is a groundbreaking devotional that fills a crucial gap by helping Christians integrate their psychedelic experiences within their faith tradition. As psychedelic therapy becomes mainstream, resources like this will be essential for the millions who encounter the Divine through these profound medicines."

-Rick Doblin, PhD, Founder and President of the Multidisciplinary Association of Psychedelic Studies (MAPS)

"Every pastor knows congregants are having experiences they can't share in church. This devotional breaks that silence with wisdom, honesty, and deep faith. By bringing mystical experience into dialogue with Gospel readings, *Beyond Words* show us how to hold both ancient tradition and emerging revelation. A gift for anyone ministering to seekers in our changing spiritual landscape."

-Rev. Molly Phinney Baskette, United Church of Christ Pastor and Author of Real Good Church

"For too long, the church has approached psychedelics with the same tepid centrism that kills every prophetic movement, either wholesale condemnation or breathless exoticism. This book does neither. Instead, *Beyond Words* offers what we desperately need: twenty-seven Christian voices who've stopped pretending that eating God on Sunday morning is somehow less radical than encountering the Divine through sacred medicines.

This isn't another attempt to baptize indigenous practices at the point of a publishing contract. It's Christians finally telling the truth about experiences many of us have been having in secret, experiences as central to our faith as Paul's Damascus road or Peter's transfiguration.

As I wrestled with whether to preach about these matters from my own pulpit, I kept returning to my ordinal vows: to minister impartially to the needs of all. This book embodies that holy obligation. It refuses to let our people suffer in silence, caught between their mystical encounters and their Sunday faith.

If the Philokalia can provide a roadmap for Orthodox mystics across centuries, then *Beyond Words* offers something equally vital: a weekly companion for those of us navigating the psychedelic renaissance while remaining rooted in the Gospel. It's medicine for a church that has forgotten how weird and wonderful our own traditions already are."

-*Rev. Nathan Dannison*, *Senior Minister, Fountain Street Church, Grand Rapids, Michigan*

"Karl Rahner famously said 'the Christian of the future will be a mystic or will not exist.' Psychedelic researchers like Walter Pahnke and William Richards have demonstrated what indigenous healers have known for millennia: that entheogenic plants can evoke meaningful and transformational mystical experiences. But it takes more than an experience to live a mystical life: for Christians, meaningful spirituality emerges from a life of prayer and spiritual practice. Which brings us to this wonderful book by Matt Zemon and an amazing array of psychedelically-informed Christian clergy and writers. On the surface, *Beyond Words* is an excellent, spiritually-oriented commentary on the Gospel Readings for Lectionary Year A. But because it invites us into meeting the wisdom of the Gospels in the light of sacred plants, it also offers a way to reclaim a truly contemplative and deeply mystical pathway into the wisdom of the Word. The end result is *Beyond Words* not only provides beautiful new insights into the Lectionary, but also makes the case for psychedelics as a gift to Christian spirituality — and an excellent resource for those of us who agree with Rahner and want to see Christians reclaim the depth, genius and beauty of the mystical element of our faith. All this to say, this is a wonderful resource that I know I will return to again and again.

-Carl McColman, author of Read the Bible Like a Mystic and The New Big Book of Christian Mysticism

"Our ancestors knew—long before theologians argued over doctrine—that Creator speaks through all forms of life. The plant teachers, dismissed for centuries by Western Christianity as 'pagan,' have always carried revelation for those with the courage to listen. *Beyond Words* is not merely a book; it is an act of sacred restoration. It calls colonial Christianity back into right relationship with the Earth and with the Indigenous knowing that was never lost: the medicine wheel and the cross are two expressions of the same Divine Intelligence, two gateways into the One Great Mystery.

These teachings honor the ancient paths while walking the Jesus road with spiritual maturity and unflinching truth. For Native Christians who have always held these worlds together in their bones—and for settlers willing to purify, decolonize, and reclaim their most authentic spiritual inheritance—Beyond Words offers a clear, initiatory path forward. It is a work of healing, remembrance, and spiritual authority."

-Norma J. Burton, MA, M.Div. Founder, Journey to Completion & the International Alliance for Spirit at Work; Unity Church minister. Norma apprenticed with Huichol mara'akame shamans of Mexico; Candomblé–Espíritu healers of Brazil; Shugendō mountain ascetics of Japan; and Cherokee, Iroquois, Hopi, and Navajo medicine holders of North America.

"In my decades of guiding psychedelic experiences and studying mystical encounters, I've witnessed countless persons seeking to integrate powerful spiritual openings with their Christian faith. This devotional beautifully contributes to that process. These pioneering voices demonstrate that the perennial wisdom revealed in transcendental states of consciousness can enrich our understanding of the Gospels. For anyone seeking to understand how mystical experiences and Christian traditions can dance together in harmony, *Beyond Words* offers both theological grounding and practical guidance."

-**William A. Richards**, *Ph.D., Author of Sacred Knowledge:*
Psychedelics & Religious Experiences

BEYOND WORDS

52 WEEKS OF GOSPEL REFLECTIONS AND
INTEGRATION PRACTICES FROM SPIRITUAL
LEADERS BRIDGING PSYCHEDELIC EXPERIENCE
AND CHRISTIAN FAITH

MATT ZEMON

FEATURING

27 VOICES FROM 15 CHRISTIAN TRADITIONS

PSYCHED
PUBLISHING

CONTRIBUTORS

Dr. Jamie Beachy - MDiv, PhD, Mennonite

Rev. Kerra Becker English - Presbyterian

Rev. Thom Belote - Unitarian Universalist

Rev. Wendy D. Cliff - Episcopal Church

Dr. Jessica Felix Romero, Ph.D. - National Faith Leader

Rev. Dr. Paul D. Fromberg - Episcopal Church

Rev. Megan Hollaway - Episcopal

Doug Hoover, D.Min. - Retired Presbyterian Army Chaplain

Paul Indorf - Religious Society of Friends (Quaker)

Rev. Pat Jobe - Unitarian Universalist

Rev. Dr. Seth D. Jones - Congregational Church

Rev. James Kress, M.A., D.D. - Senior Minister of Unity Center for Spiritual Growth

Rev. Dr. Cynthia Ramirez Lindenmeyer - Center for Spiritual Living

Dr. Bryan David McCarthy, D.Phil. - Roman Catholic

Rev. James (Jimmy) P. Marsh, Jr. - United Methodist Church

Rev. Jonathan Myers - Priest in the Episcopal Church

Rev. Ruben Nuño - Church of the Living Hope, UCC

Rev. Betsy Ouellette-Zierden, MDiv - United Methodist

Jan Owen, M.A., LPC - LPC and Baptist Minister

Hunt Priest, M.Div. - M.Div. Former Episcopal Priest

Rev. Dr. Brian Rajcok - Evangelical Lutheran Church in America

The Very Reverend Dr. Geoffrey Ready - Orthodox Church

Rev. Brent A. Reynolds - Vine Contemplative Community + Tribe of the Open Heart

Rev. Dr. Andrea F. Smith - United Methodist

Rev. Dr. Timothy Tutt - United Church of Christ

Rev. B. Jeffrey Vidt, MAT, MAR, RP - United Church of Christ

Rev. Roger Wolsey - United Methodist Church, Spiritual Director

Published by Psyched Publishing.

All rights reserved.

Copyright © 2025 by Matt Zemon

No part of this publication may be reproduced, distributed, or transmitted in any form or by any means, including photocopying, recording, or other electronic or mechanical methods, without the prior written permission of the publisher, except in the case of brief quotations embodied in critical reviews and certain other noncommercial uses permitted by copyright law. For permission requests, write to the publisher at the address below.

Name: Matt Zemon, Author

Title: Beyond Words: *52 Weeks of Gospel Reflections and Integration Practices from Spiritual Leaders Bridging Psychedelic Experience and Christian Faith*

Edited by: Melissa Zemon

ISBN: 979-8-9918940-9-8 (hardcover)
ISBN: 979-8-9939340-0-6 (paperback)

First Printed Edition: November, 2025

Psyched Publishing

www.psychedpublishing.com

Scripture quotations are from the New Revised Standard Version Updated Edition, copyright © 2021 National Council of the Churches of Christ in the United States of America. Used by permission. All rights reserved worldwide.

Brief quotations from published works are included under fair use for educational and religious commentary purposes.

TABLE OF CONTENTS

DISCLAIMERS

Risk Reduction

Entheogenic (psychedelic) use is not for everyone. The effects of entheogens can vary greatly from person to person, and some individuals may be at increased risk for adverse physical or mental health outcomes. Before considering any entheogenic practices, consult with a qualified medical or mental health professional to assess your individual risks and to decide whether this approach is appropriate for you.

Legal Disclaimer

This book explores spiritual practices and perspectives that may reference various consciousness-altering experiences. While it draws from diverse wisdom traditions and contemporary spiritual exploration, readers should be aware that certain substances mentioned in historical, religious, or experiential contexts may be controlled or illegal in their jurisdiction.

This book is intended for educational and spiritual reflection purposes only. It does not advocate for, encourage, or provide instruction on any illegal activities. Readers are responsible for understanding and complying with all applicable laws in their location.

Spiritual Practice Disclaimer

The practices and reflections in this book represent diverse approaches to Christian spiritual formation from contributors across many traditions. Some draw from contemplative practices, others from mystical theology, and many from direct spiritual experience. They are offered as invitations to explore, not prescriptions to follow.

Each person's spiritual journey is unique. Please exercise discernment and work within your own tradition, comfort level, and circumstances. If you have concerns about any practice, consult with a trusted spiritual director, pastor, or counselor.

Editorial Note

Like all spiritual writing, this book inevitably draws on the universal wisdom that belongs to no single author but flows through many voices across time. All spiritual experiences and insights shared here are authentic and drawn from lived experience. In preparing the supplemental materials, we utilized AI-based editorial tools (including OpenAI's ChatGPT, Anthropic's Claude, Perplexity, and Grammarly) as part of the writing process. These tools helped us find clearer ways to express and develop these ideas. We share this in the spirit of transparency about how books are created in our current moment.

For those who met God in the medicine and kept silent in the sanctuary.

INTRODUCTION

This book emerged from a growing community of Christians who have encountered the divine directly and found themselves looking at familiar scriptures with new eyes. After experiencing something beyond words, they wonder how to bridge their profound encounters with divine presence with the Christian faith they've known.

As seekers and believers we have studied the words, memorized the verses, and debated the theology. But after experiencing the living God, that overwhelming love and unity the scriptures describe, we return to scripture hungry for different nourishment. We want tools to integrate what we've tasted with what we've been taught.

The Gospels are, at heart, testimonies of transforming love from early disciples and communities who had encountered the Divine directly, discovering that God was not distant but intimately present in everything. Something in Jesus's presence made them feel completely open. Reality shifted. Love became a living thing they could taste and touch.

Maybe during a profound spiritual experience, in prayer, in nature, or through sacred medicine, your heart cracked open. Maybe you touched something infinite. This book is for those of us trying to make sense of that same cracking open. These pages offer a way back into the Gospel stories, as living mirrors of our own unfolding.

We'll work with body and breath, silence and speech, bringing our whole messy human selves to texts that have always been about transformation.

Each week's reflections in this 52-week journey draw from the deep wells of Christian mystical tradition, where believers throughout history have insisted that knowing *about* God differs radically from *knowing* God directly. Like the desert fathers and mothers, medieval mystics, and contemporary contemplatives, we'll approach scripture expecting to find language for what may have felt beyond words.

Some of what you read here may stretch your comfort zone. You might find language or perspectives that differ from your tradition. That's intentional. Sometimes we need fresh words to break through familiar patterns and touch the ever-new reality they attempt to describe. Like the mystics before us, we're learning that direct experience and tradition need not compete, they can dance together, each teaching us to see the other more clearly.

Matt Zemon
Chapel Hill, NC
November, 2025

HOW TO USE THIS BOOK

This book offers 52 weeks of Gospel readings paired with reflections and practices designed to move scripture from head to heart. Each week includes five elements that create a rhythm of receiving and responding:

The Reading: The Gospel passage for the week, quoted in full. Read it slowly, perhaps multiple times. Let the words settle before moving to reflection.

Through the Mystical Lens: A brief reflection written by a religious leader from various Christian traditions, approaching the text from the perspective of direct spiritual experience. These aren't traditional biblical interpretations, but invitations to see how the passage speaks to the soul's journey toward union with God.

Reflection Questions: A few questions to ponder throughout the week. Don't rush to answer them. Let them work on you like seeds in soil.

Spiritual Practice for the Week: A concrete exercise to embody the week's theme. These practices are simple enough to fit into daily life yet profound enough to shift your perspective when practiced regularly.

Journal Prompts: Sometimes our hands know truths our minds haven't yet grasped. Even if you don't consider yourself a writer, try engaging with these prompts by putting pen to paper.

Suggestions for Individual Use

- **Pick a consistent time:** Whether morning coffee or evening wind-down, regularity helps create a sacred rhythm.
- **Read the Gospel passage first:** Before reading the reflection, sit with the scripture. What speaks to you directly?
- **Don't rush:** This isn't a race. If one week's material needs two weeks, take them. The goal is an ongoing spiritual practice, not completion.
- **Keep a journal:** Track what emerges. You'll be surprised by what patterns appear over time.

Suggestions for Group Use

This book is ideal for self-organized groups seeking to explore the intersection of Christian faith and mystical experience. Consider gathering 4-8 people who share a commitment to spiritual growth and meet regularly. You might follow the liturgical year together, or simply choose readings that speak to your group's current journey. Some groups find it helpful to rotate facilitation, allowing each person to guide discussion of a reading that particularly resonates with them. Others prefer to move through the book systematically, creating a year-long journey of shared exploration. Whether you meet in homes, churches, or outdoor spaces, the key is creating a consistent, sacred container where participants feel safe to share their deepest spiritual experiences and questions.

- **Begin with silence:** Start gatherings with a few minutes of quiet to help everyone arrive fully.
- **Read the Gospel aloud:** Hearing scripture in community adds dimensions that silent reading misses.
- **Share experiences, not opinions:** Focus on how the practices affected you in concrete ways.
- **Speak from "I":** Use "I" statements rather than "we" or "you" when sharing. This keeps the focus on personal experience rather than making assumptions about others' journeys.
- **Honor the personal:** Create agreements about confidentiality. Deep sharing requires safety.
- **Resist fixing:** When someone shares a struggle, avoid offering solutions. Sometimes, witnessing is the medicine people need.

A Note on Approach

You'll notice the reflections often use language such as "medicine," "journey," and "transformation." This draws from Christianity's ancient understanding of salvation as healing and wholeness: that we are not merely saved from something, but restored to our original divine nature.

Throughout this book, you'll encounter the terms "psychedelic" and "entheogen" used interchangeably. "Entheogen," meaning "generating the divine within," recognizes that across human history, various cultures have used sacred plants and substances as pathways to encounter the Holy. This term distinguishes spiritual practice from recreational or purely therapeutic use. While many of our contributors use the more familiar term "psychedelic," both words point to the same territory: experiences that can illuminate and deepen faith. Whether a writer chooses "psychedelic," "entheogen," "sacred medicine," or "plant medicine," they are speaking of substances used with spiritual intention.

3

When we speak of healing in these pages, we refer to spiritual transformation and wholeness, not medical treatment. The ceremonial and sacred use of these substances, as discussed by our contributors, makes no medical claims and should not be confused with clinical or therapeutic applications.

These reflections come from diverse Christian clergy and religious leaders who bridge traditional faith with expanded states of consciousness. Their voices represent many denominations and approaches. Some weeks will resonate deeply with your experience; others may feel distant or challenging. This is by design. Take what serves your journey, leave what doesn't. Your spiritual path is uniquely yours. These words are meant as companions, not commanders, along the way.

A Note on Timing

This book follows Year A of the Revised Common Lectionary, drawing from Matthew's Gospel. Year A cycles through every three years (2025-2026, 2028-2029, and so on), but you needn't wait for a particular year to begin.

If your church follows the lectionary, these reflections can accompany your congregation's current journey through scripture. If not, begin whenever you feel called. Some readers start with Advent to experience the full arc from anticipation through resurrection. Others simply open to whatever week speaks to their current season. Spirit moves beyond liturgical calendars.

Trust your own rhythm. Many return to these reflections annually, discovering new layers with each cycle. Others dip in as needed, letting specific passages meet them where they are. The practices deepen with repetition but also stand alone as needed.

Future volumes will offer similar journeys through Mark (Year B) and Luke (Year C), completing the three-year lectionary cycle. Together, they'll provide multiple lenses through which to consider the Gospel's transformative wisdom.

An Invitation

However you choose to engage these readings, this book is for those who've encountered the Holy directly and are seeking to integrate that experience with their Christian faith.

You're not the first Christian to discover that the kingdom of God might be more immediate and present than you were taught. The apostles knew. The early mystics knew. The same Spirit that moved through them moves through you.

CHALLENGING ASSUMPTIONS

We are told to love our enemies and bless those who curse us. The world assumes that friends are to be loved and enemies hated.

We are told that the sun rises on the just and the unjust alike. The world considers this undiscriminating; it would like to see clouds over evil people and is offended when they go unpunished.

We are told that outcasts and harlots enter the kingdom of God before many who are perfunctorily righteous. Again unfair, the world thinks; respectable people should head the procession.

We are told that the gate to salvation is narrow. The world would prefer it to be broad.

We are told to be as carefree as birds and flowers. The world counsels prudence.

We are told that it is more difficult for the rich to enter the kingdom than for a camel to pass through a needle's eye. The world admires wealth.

We are told that the happy people are those who are meek, who weep, who are merciful and pure in heart. The world assumes that it is the rich, the powerful, and the well-born who are happy.

-Huston Smith, scholar of world religions and mysticism, *The World's Religions*

ADVENT

ADVENT 1: THE NECESSITY FOR WATCHFULNESS

The Reading

"But about that day and hour no one knows, neither the angels of heaven, nor the Son, but only the Father. For as the days of Noah were, so will be the coming of the Son of Man. For as in the days before the flood they were eating and drinking, marrying and giving in marriage, until the day Noah entered the ark, and they knew nothing until the flood came and swept them all away, so, too, will be the coming of the Son of Man. Then two will be in the field; one will be taken, and one will be left. Two women will be grinding meal together; one will be taken, and one will be left. Keep awake, therefore, for you do not know on what day your Lord is coming. But understand this: if the owner of the house had known in what part of the night the thief was coming, he would have stayed awake and would not have let his house be broken into.

Therefore you also must be ready, for the Son of Man is coming at an hour you do not expect.

-Matthew 24:36–44

Through the Mystical Lens

Matthew's description of God's judgment falls within a broader teaching about Christ's return after his resurrection. The language of judgment feels jarring in its foretelling of neighbors disappearing suddenly while others are left behind to face a catastrophic apocalypse, as in the time of Noah. Yet from a mystical view, divine judgment is not a final condemnation, abandonment, or apocalypse but a destruction of the old and a turning toward a portal to a radically different reality. Entheogenic prayer can bring about such sudden shifts in perception and awareness.

The question Matthew poses to his readers: How can Christians prepare for the breaking through of divine inspiration and presence, that may come as a thief in the night, stealing our rigid ideas and attachments to outdated perceptions and ways of being? This call to awakening may require a new way of being in the world where the ordinary world remains, but is now seen as it truly is—suffused with a radically revised meaning as if the world was born anew, and infused with divinity.

-Jamie Beachy, MDiv, PhD, Mennonite

Reflection Questions

1. Jamie asks why Jesus's arrival is described as "a thief in the night." What rigid ideas or attachments might need to be "stolen" from you for divine reality to break through?
2. The reflection describes the world "seen as it truly is— suffused with a radically revised meaning." When have you

experienced ordinary reality suddenly revealing itself as sacred? What had to be released for this seeing?

3. How do you balance preparing for divine breakthrough with allowing it to arrive unexpectedly? What practices help you stay open without grasping?

Spiritual Practice for the Week

This week, practice "Awakened Watchfulness":

Drawing from the Mennonite and Amish traditions that value silence, commit to 10 minutes of meditation each morning. Sit comfortably and breathe naturally.

Instead of waiting for something to happen, rest in what Jamie calls "present moment awareness as an arising reality." Notice how each moment is already complete, already arriving.

Throughout the day, when you catch yourself living in the past or future, pause and ask: "What if this ordinary moment is the breaking through?" Feel how the divine might already be here, disguised as the everyday.

Before going to sleep, reflect: Where did I notice the sacred hidden in plain sight today? What "thief in the night" moments stole my expectations and left truth?

Journal Prompts

Jamie describes divine judgment as "destruction of the old and a turning toward a portal to a radically different reality." Write about a time when loss became a portal. What apocalypse in your life revealed itself as birth?

The reflection asks how we can "prepare for the breaking through of divine inspiration." Describe a moment when spiritual insight arrived like a thief: sudden, disruptive, taking what you thought you knew. How do you now live differently, knowing such visitations are possible?

ADVENT 2: THE PROCLAMATION OF JOHN THE BAPTIST

The Reading

In those days John the Baptist appeared in the wilderness of
Judea, proclaiming, "Repent, for the kingdom of heaven has
come near." This is the one of whom the prophet Isaiah spoke
when he said,

The voice of one crying out in the wilderness:
'Prepare the way of the Lord;
    make his paths straight.'

Now John wore clothing of camel's hair with a leather belt
around his waist, and his food was locusts and wild honey.
Then Jerusalem and all Judea and all the region around the
Jordan were going out to him, and they were baptized by him
in the River Jordan, confessing their sins.

But when he saw many of the Pharisees and Sadducees
coming for his baptism, he said to them, "You brood of vipers!
Who warned you to flee from the coming wrath? Therefore,
bear fruit worthy of repentance, and do not presume to say to
yourselves, 'We have Abraham as our ancestor,' for I tell you,

God is able from these stones to raise up children to Abraham. Even now the ax is lying at the root of the trees; therefore every tree that does not bear good fruit will be cut down and thrown into the fire.

"I baptize you with water for repentance, but the one who is coming after me is more powerful than I, and I am not worthy to carry his sandals. He will baptize you with the Holy Spirit and fire. His winnowing fork is in his hand, and he will clear his threshing floor and will gather his wheat into the granary, but the chaff he will burn with unquenchable fire."

-Matthew 3:1–12

Through the Mystical Lens

There's an uncomfortable tension in this story about who gets access to the ritual of baptism and who doesn't. I come from a tradition that baptizes infants, so the idea that the grace bestowed by baptism requires a prerequisite life change makes me a bit squeamish. Yet when I read it through the mystical lens, it makes sense. The draw to the wilderness, the unpredictability, the unmerited openness and wonder of the spiritual journey is held in contrast to the stable, predictable, closed canon of religious authority. Those sullied by the suffering of everyday life came to John the Baptist in droves from all over the region. These pilgrims were welcomed. They were immersed in the sacred waters of the Jordan river, and rising up, they discovered an awareness of God as near to them as their very next breath.

However, when the Pharisees and Sadducees make the trek to the wilderness, John questions their motives. He calls them snakes. He tells them that their heritage and tradition are nothing compared to the fruit that is worthy of repentance. This truth had to hurt.

John reminds the outwardly religious that an inner spiritual transformation involves necessary pruning, The ax is lying at the root of the trees and those not bearing good fruit will be thrown into the fire. To be transformed, it becomes necessary to "let go." Perhaps John could see that the religious leaders were holding on too tightly to their righteous halos. They would have to let go of their old life, forsake their tradition, and break from the inherited patterns of their ancestors to open up and encounter God's presence.

John preached repentance and little else. For those who were ready to come face to face with their real selves - this water baptism symbolized their courage to walk into the wilderness and be blessed by something so unusual, so crazy as to be life-changing. It also refocused their eyes to behold the fire and the Spirit yet to come. For those who were only looking for a chance to disparage the nutter in the camel-hair coat, they received a rebuke, and were turned away as they put back on the masks of their religiosity.

-Rev. Kerra Becker English, Presbyterian

Reflection Questions

1. John challenged religious leaders who came seeking baptism without inner transformation. When have you witnessed the difference between performing spiritual practices and truly surrendering to them?
2. The reflection contrasts those "ready to come face to face with their real selves" with those seeking to "disparage the nutter in the camel-hair coat." When have you felt truly ready for transformation versus merely curious about a spiritual practice?
3. Kerra suggests that repentance "divides those who will soften their hearts to their own truth from those who turn them into stone." How do you prepare your heart for deep spiritual work, whether in meditation, ceremony, or daily life?

Spiritual Practice for the Week

This week, practice preparing your heart for encounter with the sacred. Each morning, sit quietly and place your hand on your chest. Feel the rhythm of your heartbeat: steady, persistent, alive.

Ask yourself: "What truth about myself am I resisting today?" Listen without judgment. Notice if your heart feels soft and open or protected and rigid.

Breathe into whatever arises. If you feel hardness, don't force it open. Simply acknowledge: "This is where I am today." If you feel openness, breathe gratitude for this receptivity.

Before any spiritual practice this week (prayer, meditation, time in nature), return to this heart-check. Notice how the quality of your preparation affects the depth of your experience. The journey always reflects the readiness of the sojourner.

Journal Prompts

John wore camel hair and ate locusts, choosing radical simplicity to create space for Spirit. What complexities or comforts in your life might be crowding out deeper spiritual awareness? Explore one area where simplification might open new channels for encounter with the sacred.

Write about a time when you felt genuinely ready to receive a life-changing moment versus a time when you felt denied such transformation. What internal or external conditions created this readiness or resistance? How might you cultivate the conditions for receptivity now?

ADVENT 3: MESSENGERS FROM JOHN THE BAPTIST

The Reading

Messengers from John the Baptist

When John heard in prison what the Messiah was doing, he sent word by his disciples and said to him, "Are you the one who is to come, or are we to wait for another?" Jesus answered them, "Go and tell John what you hear and see: the blind receive their sight, the lame walk, those with a skin disease are cleansed, the deaf hear, the dead are raised, and the poor have good news brought to them. And blessed is anyone who takes no offense at me."

Jesus Praises John the Baptist

As they went away, Jesus began to speak to the crowds about John: "What did you go out into the wilderness to look at? A reed shaken by the wind? What, then, did you go out to see? Someone dressed in soft robes? Look, those who wear soft robes are in royal palaces. What, then, did you go out to see? A prophet? Yes, I tell you, and more than a prophet. This is the one about whom it is written,

'See, I am sending my messenger ahead of you,
who will prepare your way before you.'

"Truly I tell you, among those born of women no one has arisen greater than John the Baptist, yet the least in the kingdom of heaven is greater than he.

-Matthew 11:2–11

Through the Mystical Lens

In my tradition (Unitarian Universalism) I was taught to read the Bible through the lens of social justice. In this passage we may see John as a political prisoner of an oppressive empire. We may see Jesus a community organizer distributing free health care, advocating for disability rights, and creating mutual aid societies. Or something like that.

A mystical lens would help us to see this story as also about becoming free from the prisons of our perception. What new world becomes possible when we learn to heal from those things that keep us stuck? Can we heal from shame, from worry, from self-hatred, from the harmful illusion of our separateness?

Audre Lorde said that we can never dismantle the master's house by using the master's tools. Jesus says that the truth we seek will not come from someone wearing the soft robes that people in fancy palaces wear. Instead, perhaps, we can find that truth deep within ourselves, amongst each other in community, and from the great mystery that ever encircles us.

This passage from scripture ends with Jesus describing the kingdom of heaven. I imagine the kingdom of heaven to be a place of radical oneness and unity. Through a social justice lens, the kingdom of heaven is a time when hierarchies of race, sex, and class dissolve into the unity of all people. Through a mystical lens, the kingdom of heaven is an understanding that our separateness – from each other, from nature, and from the universe – is an illusion.

It is said that we need our daily bread (Matthew 6:11). It is also said that we do not live by bread alone (Matthew 4:4). We need both. And, somehow, both are one.

-Rev. Thom Belote, Unitarian Universalist

Reflection Questions

1. Thom asks, "What new world becomes possible when we learn to heal from those things that keep us stuck?" After experiencing expanded consciousness, what prisons of perception have you recognized in your own life? How has healing from these illusions changed your daily experience of reality?
2. "Through a mystical lens, the kingdom of heaven is an understanding that our separateness... is an illusion." When you've touched this unity consciousness, how do you maintain that knowing while navigating a world that insists on separation? What practices help you remember oneness when duality feels overwhelming?
3. The reflection ends with "We need both. And, somehow, both are one," referring to bread and spirit, justice and mysticism. How do you integrate your mystical insights with concrete action in the world? Where do you see the unity between inner transformation and outer service?

Spiritual Practice for the Week

Each morning this week, practice "prison recognition and release." Sit quietly for 10 minutes and ask yourself: "What prison of perception am I inhabiting today?" It might be shame, worry, self-hatred, or the illusion of separateness mentioned in the reflection.

Once you identify today's prison, breathe deeply and imagine its walls becoming transparent. You haven't escaped; you've realized the walls were never solid. They were made of thoughts, beliefs, and perceptions that seemed real but weren't ultimate truth.

Throughout your day, when you notice yourself back in that prison, pause and remember: "This separateness is an illusion." Feel how you are connected to everything around you, including the air you breathe, the ground beneath you, and the hearts of those you encounter. End by taking one small action from this place of remembered unity.

Journal Prompts

The reflection states that "the truth we seek will not come from someone wearing the soft robes that people in fancy palaces wear." Write about a time when profound truth came to you from an unexpected source: perhaps through plant medicine, from someone society overlooks, or from your own depths. How did this experience change your understanding of spiritual authority?

"I imagine the kingdom of heaven to be a place of radical oneness and unity," Thom writes, describing how hierarchies dissolve. Recall a moment in your journey when you experienced this dissolution of hierarchies, when all distinctions of better/worse, higher/lower, sacred/profane fell away. How do you carry that kingdom consciousness into a world still organized by divisions?

ADVENT 4: THE BIRTH OF JESUS THE MESSIAH

The Reading

Now the birth of Jesus the Messiah took place in this way. When his mother Mary had been engaged to Joseph, but before they lived together, she was found to be pregnant from the Holy Spirit. Her husband Joseph, being a righteous man and unwilling to expose her to public disgrace, planned to divorce her quietly. But just when he had resolved to do this, an angel of the Lord appeared to him in a dream and said, "Joseph, son of David, do not be afraid to take Mary as your wife, for the child conceived in her is from the Holy Spirit. She will bear a son, and you are to name him Jesus, for he will save his people from their sins." All this took place to fulfill what had been spoken by the Lord through the prophet:

"Look, the virgin shall become pregnant and give birth to a son,

and they shall name him Emmanuel,"

which means, "God is with us." When Joseph awoke from sleep, he did as the angel of the Lord commanded him; he took her as his wife but had no marital relations with her until she had given birth to a son, and he named him Jesus.

-Matthew 1:18–25

Through the Mystical Lens

Joseph is in a bind. Mary, his betrothed, is pregnant with a child not his own. Does he marry her and raise another man's child or "dismiss her quietly?" He cares enough about her to be "unwilling to expose her to public disgrace," but if he releases her from their engagement, as an unwed mother in those times (and often today), she faces huge economic, social, and emotional barriers and cruel judgment. He's facing an impossible decision. He's stuck. But then he has a dream.

Dreams can be like psychedelic journeys - strange visitors, surprising visions, guidance for intractable conditions, and often the sense of fear. But God's Messenger appears to Joseph and immediately calls him by name and acknowledges his lineage. Joseph and his dilemma are witnessed, seen by God. Psychedelic experiences often reveal to us our own humanness, our deepest sense of self, and sometimes tie us to our ancestors.

Then the Messenger comforts Joseph by saying, "Do not be afraid." With this three-part address, the Messenger enacts what Jesus' name foretells, "God is with us." And in the context of the problem Joseph isn't able to solve on his own, God's message is a Way where there had appeared to be no way. When working with entheogens, we are encouraged to recognize the "soul manifesting" nature of these plant medicines, of God being with and in us as we search for healing and transformation.

In Madeleine L'Engle's book about the birth of Jesus, *The Glorious Impossible*, she writes, "Possible things are easy to believe. The Glorious Impossibles are what bring joy to our hearts, hope to our lives, song to our lips." May this Advent be a time to dream, to pray, to prepare for the birth of Jesus and all the other "Glorious Impossibles" that bring about personal and collective healing and hope.

-The Reverend Wendy D. Cliff, Episcopal Church

Reflection Questions

1. Wendy writes that "Dreams can be like psychedelic journeys - strange visitors, surprising visions, guidance for intractable conditions." When have your own expanded consciousness experiences provided guidance for a situation where you felt completely stuck? How did the wisdom arrive differently than your rational mind expected?

2. The angel addresses Joseph by name, acknowledges his lineage, and says "Do not be afraid," showing that he is fully witnessed by God. During your mystical experiences, how have you felt seen and known in your fullness? What fears dissolved when you experienced being truly witnessed?

3. Wendy shares L'Engle's words about "Glorious Impossibles" that "bring joy to our hearts, hope to our lives, song to our lips." What impossible thing has become possible through your spiritual journey? How do you stay open to further impossibilities wanting to be born through you?

Spiritual Practice for the Week

Each evening this week, create space for "dream consciousness" before sleep. Sit quietly for 10 minutes and bring to mind a situation where you feel stuck between difficult choices, as Joseph was. Hold the dilemma gently without forcing a solution.

As you prepare for sleep, invite guidance through an inner prayer: "Show me the way where there appears to be no way." Keep a journal beside your bed. Upon waking, before checking your phone or engaging the day's demands, spend 5 minutes recording any dreams, feelings, or insights that arose.

Like Joseph, practice trusting the guidance that comes through non-ordinary states. Notice what shifts when you allow wisdom to arrive through channels beyond your rational mind. Remember that solutions often come wrapped in mystery, requiring courage to follow.

Journal Prompts

Wendy describes how "God's message is a Way where there had appeared to be no way" in Joseph's impossible situation. Write about a time when you faced what seemed like an impossible choice. How did expanded consciousness or spiritual experience reveal a third option you couldn't previously see? What had to shift in you to recognize and follow this new way?

The reflection notes how "Psychedelic experiences often reveal to us our own humanness, our deepest sense of self, and sometimes tie us to our ancestors." Explore a moment when you felt connected to your lineage or ancestral wisdom during expanded consciousness. What did you discover about who you are beyond your individual story? How does this ancestral connection inform your current path?

CHRISTMAS SEASON

CHRISTMAS EVE / CHRISTMAS DAY: THE WORD BECAME FLESH

The Reading

In the beginning was the Word, and the Word was with God, and the Word was God. He was in the beginning with God. All things came into being through him, and without him not one thing came into being. What has come into being in him was life, and the life was the light of all people. The light shines in the darkness, and the darkness did not overtake it.

There was a man sent from God whose name was John. He came as a witness to testify to the light, so that all might believe through him. He himself was not the light, but he came to testify to the light. The true light, which enlightens everyone, was coming into the world.

He was in the world, and the world came into being through him, yet the world did not know him. He came to what was his own, and his own people did not accept him. But to all who received him, who believed in his name, he gave power to become children of God, who were born, not of blood or of the will of the flesh or of the will of man, but of God.

And the Word became flesh and lived among us, and we have seen his glory, the glory as of a father's only son, full of grace and truth. (John testified to him and cried out, "This was he of whom I said, 'He who comes after me ranks ahead of me because he was before me.' ") From his fullness we have all received, grace upon grace. The law indeed was given through Moses; grace and truth came through Jesus Christ. No one has ever seen God. It is the only Son, himself God, who is close to the Father's heart, who has made him known.

-John 1:1–14

Through the Mystical Lens

"In the beginning was the Word..." Before form, before name, before the universe unfolded— pure Presence, infinite Consciousness, the Light that creates all light.

Those who've touched that primordial awareness know it intimately. Maybe in the depths of contemplative prayer. Maybe when a sacred medicine dissolved every boundary and you recognized: *This consciousness looking through my eyes is the same consciousness looking through all eyes.* The "I AM" that spoke at Sinai, speaking as you, in you, through you.

The early church fathers understood this. As Athanasius declared: "He was made man so that we might be made god." The Word didn't just visit humanity—he joined himself to it, forever. This is *theosis,* our transformation into the divine life we were always meant to share.

"The light shines in the darkness, and the darkness did not overcome it." Every mystical journey teaches this truth. When everything dissolves—your self-constructed identity, your certainties, even your sense of autonomous self—what remains? The Light remains. Love remains. The indestructible Word.

Ephrem the Syrian knew why the incarnation was necessary: Christ "used our body, so that we might endure the sight of him." At the transfiguration, the apostles glimpsed his unveiled glory and were overwhelmed. The infinite made finite. The eternal stepped into time. God clothed himself in flesh so we could bear to look upon glory.

"We have seen his glory." These aren't just words about an ancient event. This is present tense. The Word continues becoming flesh—in the Eucharist, in sacred community, in every moment we recognize Love's presence.

And the staggering promise: "To all who received him, he gave power to become children of God." Not metaphorically. Actually. The Light that shone at creation is awakening *in* you. Open the eyes of your heart, stay watchful, and prepare to meet the one who is that Light never overtaken by night.

-The Very Reverend Dr Geoffrey Ready, Orthodox Church

Reflection Questions

1. Fr Geoffrey writes of recognizing that "This consciousness looking through my eyes is the same consciousness looking through all eyes." When have you experienced this unity of awareness, whether in prayer, nature, or expanded states of consciousness?
2. The reflection states that Christ "used our body, so that we might endure the sight of him." How has embodiment, rather than escape from the body, been essential to your deepest spiritual experiences?
3. "The Word continues becoming flesh: in the Eucharist, in sacred community, in every moment we recognize Love's

presence." Where do you witness this ongoing incarnation in your daily life?

Spiritual Practice for the Week

Each day this week, practice recognizing the Word becoming flesh in the present moment.

Upon waking, before opening your eyes, rest in the awareness that exists before thought. This is the Light that was "in the beginning." Feel how this same awareness has been with you since your first memory, unchanging while everything else changes.

Throughout the day, pause when you encounter beauty, kindness, or love in nature, in another's eyes, in simple acts of care. Touch your heart and silently acknowledge: "The Word is becoming flesh here, now."

Before sleep, review the day's moments of recognition. Where did you see glory? Where did darkness seem overwhelming, yet the Light remained? Rest in gratitude that the infinite continues to meet you in finite form.

Journal Prompts

Fr Geoffrey describes theosis, our transformation into divine life. Write about a moment when you felt yourself participating in something greater than your individual self, when the boundary between human and divine seemed to thin or dissolve. How did this change your understanding of what it means to be human?

"He came to what was his own, and his own people did not accept him." Explore a time when profound truth or love appeared in your life but you initially failed to recognize or receive it. What had to shift in you before you could say "yes" to what was being offered?

FIRST SUNDAY AFTER CHRISTMAS: THE FLIGHT TO EGYPT AND RETURN

The Reading

The Escape to Egypt

Now after they had left, an angel of the Lord appeared to Joseph in a dream and said, "Get up, take the child and his mother, and flee to Egypt, and remain there until I tell you, for Herod is about to search for the child, to destroy him." Then Joseph got up, took the child and his mother by night, and went to Egypt and remained there until the death of Herod. This was to fulfill what had been spoken by the Lord through the prophet, "Out of Egypt I have called my son."

The Massacre of the Infants

When Herod saw that he had been tricked by the magi, he was infuriated, and he sent and killed all the children in and around Bethlehem who were two years old or under, according to the time that he had learned from the magi. Then what had been spoken through the prophet Jeremiah was fulfilled:

"A voice was heard in Ramah,
  wailing and loud lamentation,
Rachel weeping for her children;
  she refused to be consoled, because they are no more."

The Return from Egypt

When Herod died, an angel of the Lord suddenly appeared in a dream to Joseph in Egypt and said, "Get up, take the child and his mother, and go to the land of Israel, for those who were seeking the child's life are dead." Then Joseph got up, took the child and his mother, and went to the land of Israel. But when he heard that Archelaus was ruling Judea in place of his father Herod, he was afraid to go there. And after being warned in a dream, he went away to the district of Galilee. There he made his home in a town called Nazareth, so that what had been spoken through the prophets might be fulfilled, "He will be called a Nazarene."

-Matthew 2:13–23

Through the Mystical Lens

"When they had left [Magi], an angel of the Lord appeared in a dream …"

In the preceding verses, the Magi bring gold, frankincense, and myrrh to the Holy Family. Each of these gifts have alchemical and medicinal qualities that are associated with spiritual purification, intensifying concentration, devotion, prayer, and restful sleep. The Magi gave gifts that supported the incubation of dreams—dreams that would be central to the safety, survival, and surrendered devotion of the family. Religious and spiritual traditions from across the globe have regarded dreams as a communication medium between humans and the divine. Frankincense is still burned in the region for sacred ceremony.

Gold was used in ancient medicinal practices while frankincense and myrrh are often distilled in oils or incense. Frankincense and Myrrh have rich scents that are traditionally used to purify spiritual and religious spaces. Joseph gets the first dream to flee to Egypt *after* receiving supportive dreaming and discernment plant resins and metals into the household.

Although incense is mentioned throughout scripture, this particular association between the fragrant and alchemical gifts of the Magi and dreaming provides us the opportunity to contemplate the role of scent in entheogenic or mystical experiences. Oftentimes ceremonial guides will use scent to help someone expand their consciousness, soften into their body, or to help ground someone. Natural plant/tree elements can influence our ability to cross into the liminal realms and can activate the imaginal realm where this scripture tells us, messages can be received.

By "having been warned in a dream," Joseph enters the long tradition of dreaming and message interpretation. During entheogenic or mystical experiences, people often report receiving messages. Whether they attribute those messages directly to the ingested plant or receive messages within the experience from ancestors, nature, messengers, or the Holy Spirit, people are initiated into the spiritual practice of discernment. Within the reading, we see that each message received and subsequent action taken is in service of a prophesized occurrence. When we begin to interpret our experiences, we too can look to scripture to see how the message aligns with the long arc of the gospel and path of love. Julian of Norwich, revered 14th century Christian mystic, spent nearly 20 years meditating, reflecting, and writing her *Revelations of Divine Love*.

During this passage, we see the Joseph remains open to communication through dreams and we can imagine he had to cultivate a practice to receive them. We see that this Holy Family of refugees are not sent to another land without alchemical support needed for continued dreaming. During a time of great stress and danger, Joseph had to be receptive enough to notice the dreams. He had to have the discernment to follow the guidance. May we all remember, those who journey as refugees are carrying dreams that are sacred.

-Dr. Jessica Felix Romero

Reflection Questions

1. The reflection suggests the Magi's gifts supported "the incubation of dreams." What practices or substances in your life create space for divine communication through dreams or visions?
2. Joseph had to be "receptive enough to notice the dreams" even during great stress. When has crisis or danger actually heightened your spiritual receptivity rather than closing it down?
3. "Those who journey as refugees are carrying dreams that are sacred." How might this change how you see and support displaced people in your community?

Spiritual Practice for the Week

This week, practice "Dream Incubation and Sacred Scent":

Before sleep each night, create a simple ritual with scent. Light incense or place a drop of essential oil (frankincense, lavender, or cedar) on your pillow. As the scent fills the space, pray: "Holy One, speak to me in the language of dreams."

Keep a journal by your bed. Upon waking, before checking devices or rushing into the day, record any dreams or fragments you remember. Don't analyze yet; simply receive.

During the day, when you smell something distinctive (coffee, rain, flowers), pause and ask: "What message might be here?" Notice how scent can shift consciousness and open liminal space.

At week's end, review your dream journal with Julian of Norwich's patient discernment in mind. What patterns emerge? What might the Holy be communicating?

Journal Prompts

The reflection notes that ceremonial guides use scent to "help someone expand their consciousness, soften into their body, or to help ground someone." Write about a time when a particular smell transported you into a different state of consciousness or brought a spiritual memory flooding back. What did that liminal moment teach you?

Joseph received multiple dreams that required immediate, life-altering action. Describe a dream or vision that asked you to make a significant change. How did you discern whether to trust it? What helped you find the courage to act?

EPIPHANY

Depending on the date of Easter, not every Epiphany Sunday is used each year. This guide includes all possible readings for Year A. Your community may use some or all of these.

THE EPIPHANY (JANUARY 6): THE VISIT OF THE MAGI

The Reading

In the time of King Herod, after Jesus was born in Bethlehem of Judea, magi from the east came to Jerusalem, asking, "Where is the child who has been born king of the Jews? For we observed his star in the east and have come to pay him homage." When King Herod heard this, he was frightened, and all Jerusalem with him, and calling together all the chief priests and scribes of the people, he inquired of them where the Messiah was to be born. They told him, "In Bethlehem of Judea, for so it has been written by the prophet:

'And you, Bethlehem, in the land of Judah,
    are by no means least among the rulers of Judah,
for from you shall come a ruler
    who is to shepherd my people Israel.' "

Then Herod secretly called for the magi and learned from them the exact time when the star had appeared. Then he sent them to Bethlehem, saying, "Go and search diligently for the child, and when you have found him, bring me word so that I may also go and pay him homage." When they had heard the king, they set out, and there, ahead of them, went the star that they had seen in the east, until it stopped over the place where the child was. When they saw that the star had stopped, they were overwhelmed with joy. On entering the house, they saw the child with Mary his mother, and they knelt down and paid him homage. Then, opening their treasure chests, they offered him gifts of gold, frankincense, and myrrh. And having been warned in a dream not to return to Herod, they left for their own country by another road.

-Matthew 2:1–12

Through the Mystical Lens

What Am I Doing Here?

The question popped into my head the first time I used psychedelics in a therapeutic setting. What am I doing here? This is beyond weird. This isn't what people like me do. What am I doing here?

My story is both easy to summarize and hard to explain. I was 62 the first time I used MDMA. I'm an Episcopal priest, a gay man, an iconographer, and a person with nearly forty years of service in the church—yet still searching for healing from old wounds. In San Francisco, where I live, someone like me can easily be categorized as irrelevant. But what complicates my story—and what makes it worth telling—is the simple fact that I was still seeking healing, and willing to be led somewhere unexpected.

When I look for myself in this story, I find my companions in the magi. They were astrologers, philosophers, and seekers—strangers in a strange land. They were also profoundly naïve about the political reality around them. Still, they pursued their goal without hesitation. They stepped into Herod's court expecting direction. And Herod, arrogance embodied, was afraid—afraid of losing his fragile power.

Just as I recognize the wondering and wandering of the magi in my own experience, I also recognize Herod's fear in myself.

What about you? Where do you find yourself in this story? Each of us brings a universe of experience to both the Gospel and to work with psychedelics—our naïveté, our fear, our wonder, our trauma, our wandering. The part that draws us all, though, is the star. There it is, shining in our imagination. We see it, even if we don't yet know what it signifies or where it leads.

To find its meaning—which is to say, to find our meaning—we may need both the wisdom of strangers and the caution awakened by our inner Herod: the part of us that fears losing control. Wisdom and fear both occupy our imaginations.

Trust the star to lead you, even when it draws you into unfamiliar country. Some will see that light as a threat, others, as a promise. Both responses live within us. And when you find yourself asking, what am I doing here? listen for the deeper question that always follows: Where is God leading me now?

-The Rev. Dr. Paul D. Fromberg, Episcopal Church

Reflection Questions

1. Paul asks: "Where do you find yourself in this story?" Are you the seeking magi, fearful Herod, or perhaps Mary holding something new and vulnerable? How might you embody all these roles simultaneously?
2. The reflection speaks of needing "both the wisdom of strangers and the caution awakened by our inner Herod." When has your fear of losing control actually protected something sacred? When has it prevented necessary transformation?
3. "Trust the star to lead you, even when it draws you into unfamiliar country." What star are you following now that

makes others (or parts of yourself) ask "What are you doing here?"

Spiritual Practice for the Week

This week, practice "Following the Star into Strange Territory":

Choose a route for a meditative walk in unfamiliar territory: a neighborhood you've never explored, a trail you've avoided, even a different path through a familiar park. Walk at dawn or dusk when stars might be visible.

Before beginning, stand with open palms and ask: "Where is the child?" Let this become your walking meditation phrase, not seeking an answer but holding the question.

As you walk the unfamiliar path, notice:

- What feels threatening? What feels promising?
- When does your inner Herod whisper warnings?
- When does your inner magi surge with curiosity?

If you feel lost or uncertain, pause and repeat: "Where is the child?" Trust that the question itself is a star leading you forward.

End by standing still, feeling your feet on the ground, and asking: "Where is God leading me now?"

Journal Prompts

Paul writes of being "willing to be led somewhere unexpected" even after forty years of church service. Write about a time when extensive experience in one area didn't prevent you from being a beginner in another. How did your expertise both help and hinder your willingness to follow a new star?

The reflection notes that "some will see that light as a threat, others, as a promise. Both responses live within us." Explore a current situation where you feel both threatened and promised by the same possibility. How might acknowledging both responses help you move forward with wisdom rather than paralysis?

THE BAPTISM OF JESUS

The Reading

Then Jesus came from Galilee to John at the Jordan, to be baptized by him. John would have prevented him, saying, "I need to be baptized by you, and do you come to me?" But Jesus answered him, "Let it be so now, for it is proper for us in this way to fulfill all righteousness." Then he consented. And when Jesus had been baptized, just as he came up from the water, suddenly the heavens were opened to him and he saw God's Spirit descending like a dove and alighting on him. And a voice from the heavens said, "This is my Son, the Beloved, with whom I am well pleased."

-Matthew 3:13–17

Through the Mystical Lens

Something about it seemed out of order, even indecent. Me baptize you? If it were not out of order, the extra assurance of righteousness would have been unwarranted. I rest in the fact that even Jesus' baptism was a bit out of order, in service to a new order enabling the Spirit to descend once again. Same Spirit. New way.

What righteousness is being fulfilled when the dove's descent is not occasioned by water, but by the earth's medicine? The praise of the body–every limb, organ and cell–at first seems impossible, then indecent, then, without much protest, completely righteous.

Why do I go to receive the 'baptism' of the medicine? Certainly not because of any insufficiency in what I already have and who I already am in Christ. Certainly not because my baptism in him lacks what is necessary for salvation. I go to fulfill all righteousness. I go to commune with God in the body, in the earth, and in the heavens where, for so long, my tribe has ignored or discounted him. Or maybe we just forgot how to get there. I go because the 'tea light spirituality' that creeps in briefly every October at St. Francis' feast day is far beneath his witness and has no teeth. Or at least I was too numb to feel their bite. I go because over the years, materialism had quietly become the underbelly of my faith. Nothing wrong with the Faith, just my faith. So, I go to remember that my job is not to fix the world, but to sing with it. I go in for this 'baptism' to know my whole being–and all of creation with me–bowed down before the Holy One, and myself beloved.

-The Rev. Megan Hollaway, Episcopal

Reflection Questions

1. Megan writes of going to the medicine to "commune with God in the body, in the earth, and in the heavens where, for so long, my tribe has ignored or discounted him." Where have you found God in places your spiritual tradition might overlook or dismiss?

2. The reflection speaks of discovering "my job is not to fix the world, but to sing with it." How has this shift from fixing to singing, from controlling to participating, appeared in your own spiritual journey?

3. Jesus insisted on baptism "to fulfill all righteousness" despite John's protests. When have you followed a spiritual calling that seemed out of order or inappropriate to others, trusting a deeper rightness?

Spiritual Practice for the Week

This week, practice recognizing the sacred in what seems "out of order."

Each morning, identify one aspect of creation you typically ignore or take for granted. Maybe it is a houseplant, the soil beneath your feet, or your own breathing body. Spend five minutes in communion with this overlooked sacred presence.

Place your hand on it (or on your heart if it's not touchable). Breathe with it. Listen not with your ears but with your whole being. What song is it singing? How can you join this song rather than trying to direct it?

Notice any discomfort with this practice. Does it feel silly? Indecent? Too earthy for proper spirituality? Stay with the discomfort, remembering that even Jesus's baptism seemed improper at first.

End by whispering: "You too are beloved." Notice how this recognition changes your relationship with the world throughout your day.

Journal Prompts

Megan confesses that "materialism had quietly become the underbelly of my faith." Examine your own spiritual life with gentle honesty. What has crept in as an "underbelly"? Perhaps intellectualism, perfectionism, or spiritual bypassing? How might returning to embodied, earthy practices restore balance?

Write about a time when you experienced "the praise of the body, every limb, organ and cell." Whether through dance, breathwork, medicine ceremony, or simple presence, when has your physical being itself become prayer? How did this somatic praise differ from mental or emotional worship?

EPIPHANY 2: THE LAMB OF GOD AND THE FIRST DISCIPLES

The Reading

The Lamb of God

The next day he saw Jesus coming toward him and declared, "Here is the Lamb of God who takes away the sin of the world! This is he of whom I said, 'After me comes a man who ranks ahead of me because he was before me.' I myself did not know him, but I came baptizing with water for this reason, that he might be revealed to Israel." And John testified, "I saw the Spirit descending from heaven like a dove, and it remained on him. I myself did not know him, but the one who sent me to baptize with water said to me, 'He on whom you see the Spirit descend and remain is the one who baptizes with the Holy Spirit.' And I myself have seen and have testified that this is the Chosen One."

The First Disciples of Jesus

The next day John again was standing with two of his disciples, and as he watched Jesus walk by he exclaimed,

"Look, here is the Lamb of God!" The two disciples heard him say this, and they followed Jesus. When Jesus turned and saw them following, he said to them, "What are you looking for?" They said to him, "Rabbi" (which translated means Teacher), "where are you staying?" He said to them, "Come and see." They came and saw where he was staying, and they remained with him that day. It was about four o'clock in the afternoon. One of the two who heard John speak and followed him was Andrew, Simon Peter's brother. He first found his brother Simon and said to him, "We have found the Messiah" (which is translated Anointed). He brought Simon to Jesus, who looked at him and said, "You are Simon son of John. You are to be called Cephas" (which is translated Peter).

-John 1:29–42

Through the Mystical Lens

John the Baptist had a calling - to announce the arrival of the Son of God. While Jesus initially appeared to him as a normal man it was a sign from God that distinguished Him from the rest. John "saw" the Spirit of God descend upon and remain on Jesus. With this knowledge, John told others, his own disciples, "The Lamb of God" is here. Two of his own disciples, desiring greater knowledge and closeness to God believed John and followed after Jesus. Surely already knowing their intention, Jesus reached out to them saying, "what are you looking for?" Their response at first seems a little odd, or vague, "where are you staying?" They were not looking for a quick healing or other prayer request, but something much deeper. They desired to abide with Him, to spend time with The Lamb of God – to know, to understand God. So Jesus, knowing the intention of their hearts invited them in, "Come and See." They had just received the ultimate invitation – "Come, and your spiritual eyes will be opened". Andrew did "see", and was compelled to tell others, beginning with his brother Peter. And, the rest is history.

The question Jesus asked Andrew and the other disciple, "what do you want, (what is your intention)?" is the same He asks us. God continues to ask every one of us at all times. And, if we desire to know Him better, to abide with Him, His response also remains the same, "Come and see". The choice is ours, and if we choose to "Come and see" He gives us sight. And with sight, we see Him everywhere – in the trees, in the smile of a child, in the face of a stranger, in the sound of our breath, in the grief in our own heart – everywhere. "Ask, and it shall be given you; seek, and ye shall find; knock, and it shall be opened unto you." May we each be blessed with these intentions and this sight.

-Doug Hoover, D.Min. - Retired Presbyterian Army Chaplain

Reflection Questions

1. Doug notes that the disciples weren't seeking "a quick healing or other prayer request, but something much deeper." What is the difference between seeking spiritual experiences and seeking to abide with the Divine itself?
2. John recognized Jesus through a mystical sign: the Spirit descending and remaining. What signs or experiences have helped you recognize the sacred presence in unexpected people or places?
3. The reflection promises that with spiritual sight, we see God "everywhere – in the trees, in the smile of a child, in the face of a stranger, in the sound of our breath, in the grief in our own heart." Which of these locations for the divine is easiest for you to perceive? Which is most challenging?

Spiritual Practice for the Week

This week, practice the invitation to "Come and see" through sacred pausing.

Set a gentle timer for three random moments each day. When it sounds, stop whatever you're doing and ask yourself: "What am I looking for in this moment?" Listen honestly. Are you seeking distraction, completion, connection, peace?

Then shift the question: "Where is the Holy One staying right here?" Look around with soft eyes. The divine might be abiding in the texture of light on the wall, in the feeling of air entering your lungs, in the weight of your body on the earth.

Spend one full minute simply seeing what's actually present. Don't search for the spectacular, often the Spirit remains on the ordinary, making it luminous. End by whispering "I see you" to whatever sacred presence you've noticed.

Journal Prompts

The disciples asked Jesus "where are you staying?" implying they wanted extended time, not just a momentary encounter. Describe a period in your life when you moved from seeking peak spiritual experiences to desiring sustained presence with the sacred. What shifted this longing in you?

Andrew immediately went to find his brother after encountering Jesus, compelled to share what he had "seen." Write about a time when spiritual sight came to you so clearly that you felt moved to tell someone. How did you translate mystical recognition into words? If you held back from sharing, explore what stopped you.

EPIPHANY 3: THE CALLING OF THE FIRST DISCIPLES

The Reading

Jesus Begins His Ministry in Galilee

Now when Jesus heard that John had been arrested, he withdrew to Galilee. He left Nazareth and made his home in Capernaum by the sea, in the territory of Zebulun and Naphtali, so that what had been spoken through the prophet Isaiah might be fulfilled:

"Land of Zebulun, land of Naphtali,
   on the road by the sea, across the Jordan, Galilee of the gentiles—
   the people who sat in darkness
      have seen a great light,
   and for those who sat in the region and shadow of death
      light has dawned."

From that time Jesus began to proclaim, "Repent, for the kingdom of heaven has come near."

Jesus Calls the First Disciples

As he walked by the Sea of Galilee, he saw two brothers,
Simon, who is called Peter, and Andrew his brother, casting a
net into the sea—for they were fishers. And he said to them,
"Follow me, and I will make you fishers of people."
Immediately they left their nets and followed him. As he went
from there, he saw two other brothers, James son of Zebedee
and his brother John, in the boat with their father Zebedee,
mending their nets, and he called them. Immediately they left
the boat and their father and followed him.

Jesus Ministers to Crowds of People
Jesus went throughout all Galilee, teaching in their
synagogues and proclaiming the good news of the kingdom
and curing every disease and every sickness among the
people.

-Matthew 4:12–23

Through the Mystical Lens

One of my great personal insights during my first session for the
Johns Hopkins clergy and spiritual leaders' psychedelic study was
that consensus reality is there because we need it. Consensus reality
is, as Terrance McKenna says, "nothing more than a culturally
sanctioned and linguistically reinforced hallucination". However, it
doesn't matter if we see through the consensus reality during an
extraordinary spiritual experience or a psychedelic trip. Consensus
reality always returns. The challenge of seeing through is not
'othering' those who have not seen through consensus reality. When
'the people who lived in darkness' see 'a great light', it is easy to
remove oneself from the world 'they' live in.

When I lived in New York City, I became part of a psychedelic group
whose tagline was "Find the Others". Most who gathered were glad
to find people who had a shared experience with another. A few,

though, were prophets of the new psychedelic world that was about to happen. The world would finally 'wake up' and discover the illusion we lived under, they said.

'Waking up' is an ancient idea. In the New Age 1990s, 'wake up' was the watch phrase. Those who were awake could tell who was asleep. Even Jesus tells us to 'wake up' sometimes as well. But Jesus calls us deeper into the common, consensus, gritty experience of the people, not out of it. Jesus calls us to wake up to who we are meant to be when we realize we are with 'the others', those whom we have 'othered' in our desire to make ourselves different from 'those who are in darkness', those 'who have not seen what I have seen'. The true waking up in the way of Jesus is never forgetting we are also the people who were in darkness.

Jesus says to those who follow him, "I will make you fishers of people". This means we have to go to where the people are, to swim in their waters, and throw the net knowing we will get caught up in the same net we just threw.

-Rev. Dr. Seth Jones, Congregational Church

Reflection Questions

1. Seth warns against "othering those who have not seen through consensus reality." When have you used your spiritual insights to feel superior rather than more connected? How might recognizing yourself in "those who are in darkness" change your approach?
2. The reflection emphasizes going "deeper into the common, consensus, gritty experience of the people, not out of it." How do you balance honoring your mystical experiences while staying grounded in everyday shared reality?
3. Seth writes that throwing the net means "knowing we will get caught up in the same net we just threw." What happens

when you realize you're not the fisherman standing apart but also one swimming in the same waters?

Spiritual Practice for the Week

This week, practice "Recognizing Yourself in the Darkness":

Make a list of five people who trigger judgment in you: those you see as "asleep," "unconscious," or "in darkness." Next to each name, write what specific darkness you perceive in them.

Now comes the real practice: For each darkness you've identified, ask yourself: "Where does this same darkness live in me?" Be ruthlessly honest. That spiritual pride you see in another? That unconscious behavior? That resistance to growth? Find it in yourself.

Throughout the week, when you catch yourself thinking someone else needs to "wake up," pause and ask: "What am I not seeing about my own sleep?"

End each day by naming one way you discovered yourself in those you were tempted to other.

Journal Prompts

Seth shares how some in his psychedelic group became "prophets of the new psychedelic world," certain everyone else needed to wake up. Write about a time when your spiritual experiences led you to feel separate from rather than connected to others. How did you eventually find your way back to common ground?

The reflection ends with the image of getting "caught up in the same net we just threw." Describe a moment when you tried to "help" or "awaken" others, only to discover you were wrestling with the same unconsciousness. What did this mutual entanglement teach you about the illusion of spiritual hierarchy?

EPIPHANY 4:
THE BEATITUDES

The Reading

When Jesus saw the crowds, he went up the mountain, and after he sat down, his disciples came to him. And he began to speak and taught them, saying:

"Blessed are the poor in spirit, for theirs is the kingdom of heaven.

"Blessed are those who mourn, for they will be comforted.

"Blessed are the meek, for they will inherit the earth.

"Blessed are those who hunger and thirst for righteousness, for they will be filled.

"Blessed are the merciful, for they will receive mercy.

"Blessed are the pure in heart, for they will see God.

"Blessed are the peacemakers, for they will be called children of God.

"Blessed are those who are persecuted for the sake of righteousness, for theirs is the kingdom of heaven.

"Blessed are you when people revile you and persecute you and utter all kinds of evil against you falsely on my account.

Rejoice and be glad, for your reward is great in heaven, for in the same way they persecuted the prophets who were before you.

-Matthew 5:1–12

Through the Mystical Lens

A mystical experience is, among many things, something that words cannot describe. And yet, here I am, attempting to reflect on these mystical sayings of Jesus with words!

It never ceases to amaze me how words are interpreted differently. And I am further amazed at how interpretations evolve with mystical experiences.

For the first 28 years of my career, I was a pastor in the conservative, fundamentalist, evangelical church. I was trained at Liberty Baptist Theological Seminary in Lynchburg, VA. There, I was taught the literal, grammatical, historical interpretation of Scripture. And the crazy thing is, the more I leaned into that hermeneutic, the more I was drawn to where I am today, a Minister at a Unity Church in north Idaho! I never lost my faith. I have continued to find my faith and, in many cases, discover that my faith found me.

I think the blessings Jesus lists in this reading are not future blessings that will be realized in a place called heaven that a few select, chosen people will go to after they die. I think heaven is not only (maybe) a place people go after they die, but a place all people awaken and live from, today, in this present moment. I further think these so-called beatitudes outline the nuance between having faith in Jesus and having the faith of Jesus. Furthermore, I think much of modern Christianity (which I don't believe Jesus came to establish) has conflated following and learning from Jesus into worshiping him as a savior and god. In short, Jesus is a Great Example, not the Great Exception.

Thus, I think these sayings reflect more than a 'kingdom' where 'Jesus reigns', but a Realm of Love that already lives in each of us, and we remember and reconnect to Love along the adventurous path of mercy and grace. Love is not something to get or deserve. Love is something to claim and receive. Love is not imposed. It is offered. These sayings are like a guide that connects us to the fulness and completeness of Love that is already here inside of you and all creation. As Richard Rohr says, "What God loves, God becomes."

Thus, we can receive and let these sayings wash over and through us. My invitation to you today is not to read these sayings, but let these sayings read you. Can you allow them to comfort and disrupt, disorient, your life? Can you notice, with open, curious, non-judging loving presence, which passages comfort you, and which passages disturb you? Pay gentle attention to your body and maybe notice where these sayings live in your body. God's love is always breaking out of the containers we make for it, so can you notice those edges where Love is breaking your life, and your heart, open? Maybe a particular saying can lead you home to the fullness of God and Love that is already in your heart.

As one of my favorite shamans, Armand Bytton, says, "When your heart is open, you don't need to know the rules. You create them." Today, may your heart be open and (re) created by these sacred words of Jesus.

-James Kress, M.A., D.D., Senior Minister, Unity Center of Spiritual Growth

Reflection Questions

1. James invites us to let the Beatitudes "read you" rather than reading them. Which blessing most comforts you? Which most disturbs you? What does this reveal about your spiritual edges?

2. The reflection suggests heaven is "a place all people awaken and live from, today." When have you tasted this present-moment heaven? What opened that doorway?

3. James writes about "the nuance between having faith in Jesus and having the faith of Jesus." How might adopting Jesus's way of seeing rather than beliefs about him transform your spiritual practice?

Spiritual Practice for the Week

This week, practice "Being Read by the Beatitudes":

Each morning, slowly read one Beatitude aloud. Then close your eyes and notice:

- Where do these words land in your body?
- What sensations arise (tightness, warmth, resistance, opening)?
- Which parts of you feel blessed? Which feel challenged?

Don't analyze; simply notice with what James calls "open, curious, non-judging loving presence."

Throughout the day, carry your morning Beatitude like a companion. When you encounter poverty of spirit, mourning, hunger for justice, or persecution, pause and remember: "Blessed." See if you can glimpse the kingdom already present in these experiences.

Each evening, journal briefly: How did this blessing read me today? Where did I notice Love breaking out of the containers I made for it?

Journal Prompts

James shares his journey from fundamentalist training to Unity ministry, saying "I never lost my faith...my faith found me." Write about a time when your spiritual understanding underwent radical transformation. What had to break open for a larger Love to find you?

The reflection quotes: "When your heart is open, you don't need to know the rules. You create them." Describe a moment when an open heart led you beyond religious rules into creative love. What new way of being emerged from that freedom?

EPIPHANY 5: SALT, LIGHT, AND THE FULFILLMENT OF THE LAW

The Reading

Salt and Light

"You are the salt of the earth, but if salt has lost its taste, how can its saltiness be restored? It is no longer good for anything but is thrown out and trampled under foot.

"You are the light of the world. A city built on a hill cannot be hid. People do not light a lamp and put it under the bushel basket; rather, they put it on the lampstand, and it gives light to all in the house. In the same way, let your light shine before others, so that they may see your good works and give glory to your Father in heaven.

The Law and the Prophets

"Do not think that I have come to abolish the Law or the Prophets; I have come not to abolish but to fulfill. For truly I tell you, until heaven and earth pass away, not one letter, not one stroke of a letter, will pass from the law until all is accomplished. Therefore, whoever breaks one of the least of these commandments and teaches others to do the same will be called least in the kingdom of heaven, but whoever does them and teaches them will be called great in the kingdom of heaven. For I tell you, unless your righteousness exceeds that of the scribes and Pharisees, you will never enter the kingdom of heaven.

-Matthew 5:13–20

Through the Mystical Lens

Something magical happens after the ego dissolves in a psychedelic journey: an awareness awakens of the Divine within that is not chained to the limiting beliefs of the doctrine of original sin, but is grounded in a remembering of our holy origin. If I've learned anything from plant medicine, it's that the experience consistently illuminates an inner knowing that is always present yet often overshadowed by my tendency to value what I perceive outside myself rather than what dwells within.

This experience with psychedelics offers the dependability of salt, which no matter how one tries to dilute it, the potential to flavor and preserve remains inherent. Similarly, the sacred potential of psychedelics cannot truly be lost but can be distorted or suppressed by those who might be suspicious of their power. Psychedelics, when used reverently, offer the potential to expand our consciousness to where truth is revealed and preserved. Psychedelics awaken consciousness to what was always whole, the Christ presence within, drawing out the hidden divine essence that connects us all.

In this sense, psychedelics "season" consciousness not by adding anything foreign, but by dissolving illusions of separation. They quiet the ego's noise so that the inner light can shine unobstructed. This is the "light of the world" Christ spoke of, the illumination of Divine intelligence expressing through all creation.

When the veil of division fades, we harmonize with the law of cause and effect, the Law of Mind, that Jesus fulfilled through love and awareness. This is Christ consciousness: the recognition that heaven and earth are not separate realms but one continuous field of Divine Life. In this realization, the words "until heaven and earth pass away" become fulfilled because the illusion of duality dissolves into Oneness.

Though the medicine's effects fade, the remembrance remains: I am, and you are, the salt of the earth, the light of the world. Our task is to remember and reveal this truth. To let our light shine is to live as the Law fulfilled in Love. Remember your inner radiance, the Divine consciousness that you are. This is sacred reciprocity as the natural rhythm of the universe awakens to itself!

-Rev. Dr. Cynthia Ramirez Lindenmeyer, Center for Spiritual Living

Reflection Questions

1. Cynthia writes that after ego dissolution, "an awareness awakens of the Divine within." When have you experienced this inner Divine awareness as undeniable truth rather than mere concept?
2. The reflection describes how psychedelics "quiet the ego's noise so that the inner light can shine unobstructed." What ego noise most frequently blocks your inner light? How do you quiet it?
3. Cynthia speaks of recognizing that "heaven and earth are not separate realms but one continuous field of Divine Life." How does this vision of unity challenge your daily experience of separation?

Spiritual Practice for the Week

This week, practice "From Separation to Unity, Sacred Reciprocity":

Each day, choose one news story or personal interaction where you notice "us/them" thinking arising. Pause and consciously reframe it using "we" language, remembering what Cynthia calls the "Law of Mind", that our consciousness shapes our reality.

Keep a simple tally of dualistic thinking moments. When you catch yourself in separation, breathe and remember: "This is the universe awakening to itself through me."

Each evening, reflect on how your thoughts shaped your day (cause and effect). How did unity-consciousness create different outcomes than separation-consciousness?

At week's end, notice how this practice reveals "sacred reciprocity", the natural rhythm of giving and receiving when we recognize our oneness.

Journal Prompts

Cynthia writes that psychedelics reveal "what was always whole, the Christ presence within." Describe a moment, whether through medicine work, meditation, or grace, when you remembered rather than learned your divine nature. How do you maintain this remembrance when the intensity fades?

"Salt never loses its essential nature." Reflect on a time when life circumstances seemed to strip everything away from you. What remained? What unchangeable essence did you discover at your core? How does remembering this essence serve as your anchor now?

EPIPHANY 6: TEACHINGS ON ANGER, LUST, AND INTEGRITY

The Reading

Concerning Anger

"You have heard that it was said to those of ancient times, 'You shall not murder,' and 'whoever murders shall be liable to judgment.' But I say to you that if you are angry with a brother or sister, you will be liable to judgment, and if you insult a brother or sister, you will be liable to the council, and if you say, 'You fool,' you will be liable to the hell of fire. So when you are offering your gift at the altar, if you remember that your brother or sister has something against you, leave your gift there before the altar and go; first be reconciled to your brother or sister, and then come and offer your gift. Come to terms quickly with your accuser while you are on the way to court with him, or your accuser may hand you over to the judge and the judge to the guard, and you will be thrown into prison. Truly I tell you, you will never get out until you have paid the last penny.

Concerning Adultery

"You have heard that it was said, 'You shall not commit adultery.' But I say to you that everyone who looks at a woman with lust has already committed adultery with her in his heart. If your right eye causes you to sin, tear it out and throw it away; it is better for you to lose one of your members than for your whole body to be thrown into hell. And if your right hand causes you to sin, cut it off and throw it away; it is better for you to lose one of your members than for your whole body to go into hell.

Concerning Divorce

"It was also said, 'Whoever divorces his wife, let him give her a certificate of divorce.' But I say to you that anyone who divorces his wife, except on the ground of sexual immorality, causes her to commit adultery, and whoever marries a divorced woman commits adultery.

Concerning Oaths

"Again, you have heard that it was said to those of ancient times, 'You shall not swear falsely, but carry out the vows you have made to the Lord.' But I say to you: Do not swear at all, either by heaven, for it is the throne of God, or by the earth, for it is his footstool, or by Jerusalem, for it is the city of the great King. And do not swear by your head, for you cannot make one hair white or black. Let your word be 'Yes, Yes' or 'No, No'; anything more than this comes from the evil one.

-Matthew 5:21–37

Through the Mystical Lens

This passage from Jesus' "Sermon on the Mount" contains many hard sayings. Its original hearers were used to being told to heed traditional wisdom, but, instead, Jesus used it to contravene their expectations: You have heard it said, "You shall not murder," but I say that if you are angry with or insult someone, you are guilty. You have heard it said, "You shall not commit adultery," but I say even a wandering eye is unfaithful.

Psychedelic medicines, too, are an opportunity for God to challenge our usual understandings with an otherworldly authority. Has God used them to remind you of something you still have not done, of something you still have not integrated? Is God using them, like Jesus used the traditional wisdom, to ask you to go beyond the bare minimum requirements of our law and culture?

Three times, the passage mentions hell as the consequence of a check-the-box life. "Dare we hope" that any place of eternal misery is empty? Theologians like Balthasar cautiously answer "yes," but what of the terrestrial hell that living small creates? Smoldering in thoughts of another person as worthless—the deeper sense of "fool"—brings a "hell of fire" all its own, devouring and consuming from the inside out.

Psychedelic vistas are places to notice and explore emotions like those named and implied in this passage—the fear of hellish consequences, the anger or sadness or disgust that attends divorce— as well as joy. You are always inhabiting some emotion; the key is to identify it and to keep your response simple—"Yes" or "No" and not something more that leads to destruction.

- Bryan McCarthy, Roman Catholic Church

Reflection Questions

1. Bryan asks if God has used psychedelic medicines "to remind you of something you still have not done, of something you still have not integrated?" What unfinished spiritual or relational work has been revealed to you through expanded states of consciousness?

2. The reflection describes anger creating a "hell of fire" that devours "from the inside out." When have you experienced how unchecked emotions create their own forms of suffering, and how has this recognition changed your relationship with difficult feelings?

3. Jesus repeatedly says "But I say to you," offering teachings that go beyond external compliance to inner transformation. Where in your life are you being called to move beyond "bare minimum requirements" to deeper integrity?

Spiritual Practice for the Week

This week, practice the simplicity of "Yes, Yes" or "No, No" in your inner life.

Each morning, sit quietly and scan your body and heart. What emotions are present? Don't judge them; simply name them: "Anger is here" or "Fear is here" or "Joy is here."

Throughout the day, when you notice strong emotions arising, pause and ask: "Is this feeling pointing me toward love and reconciliation (Yes) or toward separation and harm (No)?"

Before any important interaction or decision, check your motivation. Are you acting from integrity (Yes) or from hidden anger, lust, or ego (No)? Keep your response simple: no elaborate justifications, just honest recognition.

Each evening, review where you said "Yes" to love and where you said "No" to harmful impulses. Celebrate the Yes moments. For the No moments, simply note what needs reconciliation without self-condemnation.

Journal Prompts

Jesus teaches that anger and insults are as serious as murder, lust as serious as adultery. Write about a time when you discovered how thoughts and emotions you considered "harmless" were actually creating suffering for yourself or others. How did this recognition come to you?

The reflection mentions "the terrestrial hell that living small creates." Explore an area of your life where you've been living small, settling for check-the-box compliance rather than wholehearted engagement. What would it look like to live large in this area, to go beyond minimum requirements into radical love?

EPIPHANY 7: LOVE YOUR ENEMIES

The Reading

Concerning Retaliation

"You have heard that it was said, 'An eye for an eye and a tooth for a tooth.' But I say to you: Do not resist an evildoer. But if anyone strikes you on the right cheek, turn the other also, and if anyone wants to sue you and take your shirt, give your coat as well, and if anyone forces you to go one mile, go also the second mile. Give to the one who asks of you, and do not refuse anyone who wants to borrow from you.

Love for Enemies

"You have heard that it was said, 'You shall love your neighbor and hate your enemy.' But I say to you: Love your enemies and pray for those who persecute you, so that you may be children of your Father in heaven, for he makes his sun rise on the evil and on the good and sends rain on the righteous and on the unrighteous. For if you love those who love you, what reward do you have? Do not even the tax

collectors do the same? And if you greet only your brothers
and sisters, what more are you doing than others? Do not even
the gentiles do the same? Be perfect, therefore, as your
heavenly Father is perfect.

-Matthew 5:38–48

Through the Mystical Lens

It's a tall order: not simply to forgive the enemy, nor merely to accept
them, but to *embrace* them, to pray for them, to love them with the
whole heart. It asks of us the very thing we most resist, even the thing
we most recoil from.

I can imagine Spirit presenting this conundrum during a medicine
journey in all its mystical and visceral ferocity. Until not long ago, I
would meet that invitation with the familiar phrase: "Oh no… not
that!"

In the Quaker tradition, we speak of "that of God" in everyone — a
spark, an Inner Light, a kernel of the Divine that lives within all
creation. We are called to see that Light in others, even when it is dim
or obscured, and to open to that same Light within ourselves. When
we do, we can find the strength to meet hatred with compassion, to
answer injury with forgiveness, and to remove, as early Friends said,
"the occasion of all wars."

But that's not the whole story. For just as the Light dwells within us,
so too does the shadow — the places we deem forbidden, alien, or
shameful; the parts we exile, deny, or sense as "enemy". Often, the
enemies we meet in the world echo those struggles we have not yet
made peace with inside our own selves. When we encounter those
places — "Oh no… not *that!*" — can we love them too?

Perhaps Jesus is speaking here of the enemy within as well as the
more literal worldly enemy. In instructing us to "be perfect", he does
not demand flawlessness, but rather invites divine wholeness: to see

73

as God sees, to love as the Light loves, without boundary or exception.

In moments of deep spiritual opening, sometimes through the worshipful use of sacred medicines, we may glimpse this truth: that in the vast mercy of Spirit, there is no "other" left to oppose. Only the quiet knowing that love is greater than all division, and that even in the enemy, within or without, the Light still shines.

I've replaced that old saying of mine with a new one:

"Ooohh... *that.*

Thank you, Lord,

for taking me where I did not want to go."

-Paul Indorf, Philadelphia Yearly Meeting of The Society of Friends
(Quakers)

Reflection Questions

1. Paul shifts from "Oh no... not that!" to "Thank you, Lord, for taking me where I did not want to go." What resistant place in you awaits this transformation from refusal to gratitude?
2. The reflection suggests that external enemies often mirror our internal exiled parts. Who or what in the outer world most triggers you, and what might this reveal about your own shadow?
3. "In the vast mercy of Spirit, there is no 'other' left to oppose." When have you glimpsed this unity that dissolves all categories of enemy? How did it change you?

Spiritual Practice for the Week

This week, practice "Meeting the Enemy with Light":

Each morning, bring to mind someone you struggle to love: perhaps someone who has hurt you, whose values oppose yours, or who simply irritates you. Hold their image gently.

Now turn inward and ask: "What part of myself does this person mirror that I've exiled or denied?" Don't force an answer; simply hold the question with curiosity.

Place one hand on your heart. Breathe deeply and imagine the Light Paul describes dwelling both in you and in this difficult person. See it as a candle flame, steady and unextinguishable, even when obscured.

Throughout the day, when you notice anger or judgment arising toward anyone, pause and whisper: "The Light shines here too." See if you can glimpse it, even for a moment.

Before sleep, offer this prayer: "Thank you for taking me where I did not want to go."

Journal Prompts

Paul writes of replacing "Oh no... not that!" with gratitude for being taken where he didn't want to go. Chronicle your own journey with a particular inner or outer enemy. What were the stages of resistance? What finally allowed the shift toward embrace?

The reflection reframes "be perfect" as an invitation to "divine wholeness: to see as God sees, to love as the Light loves, without boundary or exception." Write about a moment when you briefly experienced this boundless vision. What dissolved? What remained? How do you carry that glimpse forward?

EPIPHANY 8: DO NOT WORRY ABOUT TOMORROW

The Reading

Serving Two Masters

"No one can serve two masters, for a slave will either hate the one and love the other or be devoted to the one and despise the other. You cannot serve God and wealth.

Do Not Worry

"Therefore I tell you, do not worry about your life, what you will eat or what you will drink, or about your body, what you will wear. Is not life more than food and the body more than clothing? Look at the birds of the air: they neither sow nor reap nor gather into barns, and yet your heavenly Father feeds them. Are you not of more value than they? And which of you by worrying can add a single hour to your span of life? And why do you worry about clothing? Consider the lilies of the field, how they grow; they neither toil nor spin, yet I tell you, even Solomon in all his glory was not clothed like one of these. But if God so clothes the grass of the field, which is alive today and tomorrow is thrown into the oven, will he not much more clothe you—you of little faith? Therefore do not worry, saying, 'What will we eat?' or 'What will we drink?' or 'What will we wear?' For it is the gentiles who seek all these things, and indeed your heavenly Father knows that you need all these things. But seek first the kingdom of God and his righteousness, and all these things will be given to you as well.

"So do not worry about tomorrow, for tomorrow will bring worries of its own. Today's trouble is enough for today.

-Matthew 6:24-34

Through the Mystical Lens

Trust is a spiritual practice. Letting go of worry and anxiety is a spiritual practice. Living in the present moment is a spiritual practice. Being attentive to the natural world is a spiritual practice.

Jesus encourages all of these things in the above passage from the Sermon on the Mount. But living the present moment or finding time to be in nature can be a challenge in the relentless busyness of the modern world. The ability to trust is not some switch we can flip at will; and letting go of anxiety and worry can feel like an impossible feat when we're feeling overwhelmed by the chaos and concerns of life. And yet, Jesus preaches these practices, not because they are easy things to check off on a spiritual to-do list, but because they are profoundly transformative and have the potential to change our lives.

A psychedelic journey confronts us with the challenge and opportunity of engaging deeply with these spiritual practices. Entering into a psychedelic journey requires trust in the face of uncertainty. The experience itself may bring us face to face with that which we most fear, challenging us to trust more deeply. Our awareness may be flooded with a jarring bombardment of intense emotion or confusing thought patterns, leaving us little choice but to let go of control and rest in the flow of whatever's happening.

Additionally, or alternatively, we may experience the gift of deep trust, peace, and joy. Whether this comes at the beginning of the journey or follows a difficult phase of cathartic release, it is a tremendous gift to see for ourselves that such a delightful state is possible. We may experience the effortless flow of joy and laughter, of love and goodwill, of peace and trust welling up from inside, so much so that old anxieties seem to fall away on their own. We may experience such alignment with the present moment that we are liberated from the concerns of time and Jesus' words about tomorrow's worries take on new meaning. Furthermore, a psychedelic journey may invite us to experience nature more deeply; gazing at the lilies of the field or witnessing the birds of the air take flight may ground us in our incarnate reality, while simultaneously offering a glimpse to the divine root of it all.

In the process of integrating a psychedelic experience, these words of Jesus can provide a foundation for reflection and encourage us to trust God in every present moment to come.

-Rev. Dr. Brian Rajcok, Evangelical Lutheran Church in America

Reflection Questions

1. Brian writes that "trust is not some switch we can flip at will." Reflect on a time when a challenging experience (psychedelic or otherwise) forced you to develop trust gradually, moment by moment. What did that process teach you?
2. The reflection mentions experiencing "such alignment with the present moment that we are liberated from the concerns of time." When have you tasted this freedom from temporal anxiety, and how do you return to that state in daily life?
3. Jesus points to birds and lilies as teachers of trust. What aspect of the natural world has most profoundly taught you about letting go of control and resting in divine provision?

Spiritual Practice for the Week

This week, practice "Consider the Lilies" meditation in three ways:

Morning: Upon waking, before checking any devices, go to a window or step outside. Find one living thing: a plant, bird, cloud, or even your own breathing body. Spend three minutes simply observing how it exists without anxiety, how it participates in the present moment completely.

Midday: When worry arises, pause and ask: "What would the lilies do?" Not as bypassing, but as genuine inquiry. The lilies don't ignore storms, they bend with them. They don't deny winter, they rest through it. How might you meet this concern with that same natural wisdom?

Evening: Before sleep, place your hand on your heart and recall one moment from the day when you experienced even a brief freedom from worry, perhaps while laughing, creating, or simply breathing. Let that moment expand in your awareness, trusting it as evidence that peace is possible.

Journal Prompts

Brian describes how psychedelic experiences can bring us "face to face with that which we most fear, challenging us to trust more deeply." Write about a time when confronting a deep fear, in any context, ultimately led to greater trust. What had to die in you for that trust to be born?

The reflection speaks of "old anxieties seeming to fall away on their own" during moments of profound alignment. Identify one persistent worry that you carry. If it were to simply fall away, what would be revealed underneath? What is this anxiety protecting you from experiencing?

TRANSFIGURATION SUNDAY: JESUS IS TRANSFIGURED ON THE MOUNTAIN

The Reading

Six days later, Jesus took with him Peter and James and his brother John and led them up a high mountain, by themselves. And he was transfigured before them, and his face shone like the sun, and his clothes became bright as light. Suddenly there appeared to them Moses and Elijah, talking with him. Then Peter said to Jesus, "Lord, it is good for us to be here; if you wish, I will set up three tents here, one for you, one for Moses, and one for Elijah." While he was still speaking, suddenly a bright cloud overshadowed them, and a voice from the cloud said, "This is my Son, the Beloved; with him I am well pleased; listen to him!" When the disciples heard this, they fell to the ground and were overcome by fear. But Jesus came and touched them, saying, "Get up and do not be afraid." And when they raised their eyes, they saw no one except Jesus himself alone.

As they were coming down the mountain, Jesus ordered

them, "Tell no one about the vision until after the Son of Man
has been raised from the dead."

-Matthew 17:1–9

Through the Mystical Lens

Friends, if there was ever a Gospel story that inherently sounded like
something one might experience on a journey with Sacred Medicines,
the story of the Transfiguration is such a scriptural psychedelic
moment. From a theological perspective, this supernatural event high
on the mountaintop - complete with visions of the ancestors
communing and engaging with us still...the audible and affirming
voice of God coming from the cloud... and most importantly Jesus,
Mary's boy who was raised in the working class neighborhood of
Nazareth, revealing himself as the Cosmic Christ clothed with
garments that transcend time and space and which are the very
elements of the universe - is an essential part of the transition from
the season of Epiphany into the season of Lent.

In the original Greek, the emotion that this experience evoked in the
disciples was "phobeo" which is translated as "fear" or "terror". I
wonder if the three disciples who had the privilege of witnessing this
extraordinary phenomenon were asking themselves whether or not
what they had just seen was real or just the "drugs" speaking?
Additionally, this mystical experience came with unusual
instructions...keep quiet, bury this revelation deep in your spirit until
you see me transfigure once again from the grave to glory for the
redemption of all humanity.

It may sound like a huge stretch, but these instructions to the disciples
after such a consciousness altering experience, sounds an awful lot like
Jesus instructing his disciples in the power that comes from integration
after one has had a life altering mystical experience. As we pivot from
the season of Epiphany to the season of Lent, how can we hold back

from shouting from the rooftops, to our loved ones, our closest friends, people that may or may not feel the same way about Sacred Medicines, that we have seen or felt something that changes everything? Yet, this transformational experience and the instructions to integration before public declaration, must be viewed like a seed. The roots of our mystical experiences MUST spread like tentacles that integrate across our mind, body and spirit...and into daily practices and a lifestyle that bears the kind of fruit that is so rich with integration that it is undeniable.

This is no small task... Climb the mountain. Experience the Glory. Do the work. Let the fruit speak for itself.

-Rev. Ruben Nuño, Church of the Living Hope UCC

Reflection Questions

1. Ruben writes that after consciousness-altering experiences, we want to shout "from the rooftops...that we have seen or felt something that changes everything." When have you struggled to contain such an experience? What helped you honor the need for integration before declaration?
2. The reflection describes how "the roots of our mystical experiences MUST spread like tentacles" through mind, body, and spirit. Where in your life is a past revelation still seeking deeper integration?
3. Jesus instructs the disciples to "tell no one about the vision" until after the resurrection. What transformative experience are you still holding in sacred silence, waiting for the right moment to share?

Spiritual Practice for the Week

This week, practice "Integration Before Declaration":

Identify one profound spiritual experience you've been eager to share. Instead of speaking about it this week, follow Jesus's instruction to the disciples: hold it in sacred silence.

Each day, spend 10 minutes quietly sitting with this experience. Ask yourself:

- How are the roots of this experience spreading through my mind, body, and spirit?
- What daily practices is this experience calling me to?
- What fruit is beginning to grow from this seed?

Throughout the week, when you feel the urge to share your experience, pause and remember Ruben's sequence: "Climb the mountain. Experience the Glory. Do the work. Let the fruit speak for itself."

By week's end, notice what has shifted through this practice of holding rather than proclaiming. Is the experience integrating more deeply? Is the eventual fruit becoming clearer?

Journal Prompts

Ruben describes the disciples experiencing "phobeo" (fear/terror) and wondering if what they saw was real or "just the drugs speaking." Write about a time when you questioned the validity of your own mystical experience. How did you eventually discern what was true? What helped you trust the revelation while also doing the integration work?

"Climb the mountain. Experience the Glory. Do the work. Let the fruit speak for itself." Trace one significant mystical experience through all four stages: the ascent (preparation), the peak experience, the integration work, and the eventual fruit. What did each stage teach you about patience and transformation?

LENT

ASH WEDNESDAY: TREASURES IN HEAVEN

The Reading

Concerning Almsgiving

"Beware of practicing your righteousness before others in order to be seen by them, for then you have no reward from your Father in heaven.

"So whenever you give alms, do not sound a trumpet before you, as the hypocrites do in the synagogues and in the streets, so that they may be praised by others. Truly I tell you, they have received their reward. But when you give alms, do not let your left hand know what your right hand is doing, so that your alms may be done in secret, and your Father who sees in secret will reward you.

Concerning Prayer

"And whenever you pray, do not be like the hypocrites, for they love to stand and pray in the synagogues and at the street corners, so that they may be seen by others. Truly I tell you, they have received their reward. But whenever you pray, go into your room and shut the door and pray to your Father who is in secret, and your Father who sees in secret will reward you.

Concerning Fasting

"And whenever you fast, do not look somber, like the hypocrites, for they mark their faces to show others that they are fasting. Truly I tell you, they have received their reward. But when you fast, put oil on your head and wash your face, so that your fasting may be seen not by others but by your Father who is in secret, and your Father who sees in secret will reward you.

Concerning Treasures

"Do not store up for yourselves treasures on earth, where moth and rust consume and where thieves break in and steal, but store up for yourselves treasures in heaven, where neither moth nor rust consumes and where thieves do not break in and steal. For where your treasure is, there your heart will be also.

Matthew 6:1–6, 16–21

Through the Mystical Lens

Matthew 6 comes in the middle of the Sermon on the Mount, where Jesus stands before the crowd naming with clarity the futility of living for show and redirecting attention toward what truly matters. His words are not whispered or shouted, but spoken with the steady force of truth — a call to return to what matters most.

On Ash Wednesday, those who gather already carry some awareness of fragility. They come to receive ashes, to wear the mark of mortality across their foreheads. "From dust you came, and to dust you shall return." We do not need to be convinced of our limits, but we do need to be reminded of how to live in the midst of them.

I remember one Ash Wednesday, early in my ministry, when our congregation still met upstairs in a small building. My father, grieving the loss of my mother with me, stood beside me to preach and to mark foreheads with ashes. We were fragile, yet grateful to be together. His frail body beside my own gave the congregation a living picture of the truth we proclaimed: life is fleeting, yet love endures.

My treasure that day was the recognition that I still had my father, that even in my mother's passing we were not alone — the congregation had gathered, and Christ was present among us. My treasure was to know my fragility, and at the same time to sense my eternal strength. This is the treasure that cannot be taken away. As Jesus says, "neither moth nor rust consumes, nor thieves break in and steal." This treasure dwells in the heart.

In prayer, meditation, and even in the mystical clarity opened by psychedelic medicine, the same lesson emerges: possessions and reputation fade, but what remains is connection — to God, to one another, to the earth.

On this day, we are called to live with love, to give with mercy, to treasure communion over accumulation. That is the treasure that endures beyond dust and ashes.

-Rev. Betsy Ouellette Zierden, United Methodist

Reflection Questions

1. Betsy writes of "the mystical clarity opened by psychedelic medicine" revealing that "possessions and reputation fade, but what remains is connection." When have your own experiences with expanded consciousness stripped away the superficial to reveal what truly endures? How has this

changed your relationship to material things and social approval?

2. The Gospel calls us to practice in secret, where only "your Father who sees" can witness. After experiencing the dissolution of ego boundaries, how do you understand this divine witnessing? What does it mean to be truly seen when the observer and observed merge into one?

3. Betsy discovered her treasure was "to know my fragility, and at the same time to sense my eternal strength." How do you hold both your human limitations and your infinite nature? What practices help you remember this paradox in daily life?

Spiritual Practice for the Week

Each morning this week, before engaging with the world, sit quietly for ten minutes in your room with the door closed, as Jesus instructs. Begin by placing your hand on your heart and feeling its steady rhythm. This is your treasure house.

Now bring to mind something you've been doing "to be seen by others": perhaps posting on social media, seeking recognition at work, or even performing spirituality. Without judgment, notice how this feels in your body. Then shift your attention to a moment of genuine connection you've experienced, whether in prayer, meditation, or expanded consciousness. Feel the difference between performing and being.

End by silently offering one secret act of kindness you'll do today, telling no one. Let this practice of hiddenness reveal where your true treasure lies.

Journal Prompts

Betsy shares the image of standing beside her grieving father on Ash Wednesday, "his frail body beside my own," giving the congregation a living picture of life's fleeting nature alongside enduring love. Write about a moment when you witnessed or experienced how fragility and strength exist together. How did this revelation come to you, and how does it inform your spiritual path?

"From dust you came, and to dust you shall return," yet Betsy affirms that connection to God, one another, and the earth endures beyond our mortality. Explore what you've discovered about what survives the dissolution of form. What have your mystical experiences taught you about what remains when everything else falls away?

LENT 1: THE TESTING OF JESUS

The Reading

Then Jesus was led up by the Spirit into the wilderness to be tested by the devil. He fasted forty days and forty nights, and afterward he was famished. The tempter came and said to him, "If you are the Son of God, command these stones to become loaves of bread." But he answered, "It is written,

'One does not live by bread alone,
but by every word that comes from the mouth of God.' "

Then the devil took him to the holy city and placed him on the pinnacle of the temple, saying to him, "If you are the Son of God, throw yourself down, for it is written,

'He will command his angels concerning you,'
and 'On their hands they will bear you up,
so that you will not dash your foot against a stone.' "

Jesus said to him, "Again it is written, 'Do not put the Lord your God to the test.' "

Again, the devil took him to a very high mountain and showed him all the kingdoms of the world and their glory, and he said to him, "All these I will give you, if you will fall down and worship me." Then Jesus said to him, "Away with you, Satan! for it is written,

'Worship the Lord your God,
and serve only him.' "

Then the devil left him, and suddenly angels came and waited on him.

-Matthew 4:1–11

Through the Mystical Lens

In this passage Jesus confronts the devil and Satan's temptation to live selfishly, to take advantage of the powers that come with being the Son of God for his own benefit. It seems to have been necessary that before his ministry began, Jesus was called to face these trials; to demonstrate undoubtedly that he was beyond the devil's influence, before he began the work of freeing others from Satan's bondage.

A central theme of the psychedelic experience is encountering our demons. Whether we are facing a terminal diagnosis, confronting depression or anxiety, coming face to face with debilitating trauma or powerful addiction, or encountering our own spiritual and existential depths, psychedelic medicine can guide us to the place where we meet our demons. Sometimes our inner demons may take the form of a nightmarish beast. We may feel fear, confusion, or overwhelming dread. Welcoming this frightening character with a sense of curiosity about what it represents and what it has to teach you is usually the most effective way forward. Such a vision may be a manifestation of your inner world, the mind's invitation to process something nightmarish in your subconscious.

Some people report that in deep psychedelic states they have encountered what feel like external presences- light or shadow, guidance or resistance. Whether these experiences reveal aspects of our own inner life or glimpses into a mystery beyond us, the invitation remains the same: to meet them with faith, not fear. In those moments, turning our attention to God's love and calling on the guidance of the Holy Spirit helps us discern what is true and move safely through whatever arises.

Whatever is encountered, maintaining an attitude of trust in God's love and guidance will also help you to discern the spirits and move through the process. Whether this nightmarish creature is an inner demon seeking to be healed or an entity beyond you altogether, an attitude of trust in God will guide us through. Such difficult experiences, like Jesus' time in the wilderness, will empower us to overcome our demons and be a force for good on behalf of others.

--Rev. Dr. Brian Rajcok, Evangelical Lutheran Church in America

Reflection Questions

1. Brian suggests that Jesus needed to demonstrate he was "beyond the devil's influence, before he began the work of freeing others." How have your own encounters with darkness or temptation prepared you to support others in their struggles?
2. The reflection distinguishes between "inner demon seeking to be healed" and external malevolent forces. How do you discern between projections of your own shadow material and genuinely harmful influences in your spiritual experiences?
3. "Welcoming this frightening character with a sense of curiosity" is suggested as a way forward. When have you transformed a terrifying experience by approaching it with curiosity rather than resistance?

Spiritual Practice for the Week

This week, practice "wilderness preparation" for encountering difficulty:

Morning Foundation: Begin each day by grounding yourself in trust. Place both feet on the floor, breathe deeply, and repeat three times: "I am held by Love that is stronger than any darkness." Feel this truth in your body before starting your day.

Midday Check-in: When you notice fear, anxiety, or temptation arising, pause and ask: "What is this trying to teach me?" Don't try to banish the feeling immediately. Instead, observe it with gentle curiosity for thirty seconds, then return to your grounding phrase.

Evening Integration: Before sleep, review any challenging encounters from the day. For each one, identify: What temptation was present (to react in anger, to escape, to despair)? How did you respond? What angels (in the form of insights, support, or grace) appeared afterward?

Practice this especially before any deep spiritual work, knowing that strength in small daily trials prepares us for larger encounters.

Journal Prompts

Write about a time when you encountered something truly frightening in a spiritual or expanded state of consciousness. How did you navigate this experience? What resources (prayer, breath, surrender, curiosity) proved most helpful? What did you learn about your own spiritual authority?

The reflection notes that "angels came and waited on him" after Jesus's ordeal. Describe a time when you emerged from a period of trial or darkness to find unexpected support or grace waiting for you. How did this experience of being "waited on" by benevolent forces change your willingness to face future challenges?

LENT 2: BORN OF WATER AND SPIRIT

The Reading

Now there was a Pharisee named Nicodemus, a leader of the
Jews. He came to Jesus by night and said to him, "Rabbi, we
know that you are a teacher who has come from God, for no
one can do these signs that you do unless God is with that
person." Jesus answered him, "Very truly, I tell you, no one
can see the kingdom of God without being born from above."
Nicodemus said to him, "How can anyone be born after
having grown old? Can one enter a second time into the
mother's womb and be born?" Jesus answered, "Very truly, I
tell you, no one can enter the kingdom of God without being
born of water and Spirit. What is born of the flesh is flesh, and
what is born of the Spirit is spirit. Do not be astonished that I
said to you, 'You must be born from above.' The wind blows
where it chooses, and you hear the sound of it, but you do not
know where it comes from or where it goes. So it is with
everyone who is born of the Spirit." Nicodemus said to him,

"How can these things be?" Jesus answered him, "Are you the teacher of Israel, and yet you do not understand these things?

"Very truly, I tell you, we speak of what we know and testify to what we have seen, yet you do not receive our testimony. If I have told you about earthly things and you do not believe, how can you believe if I tell you about heavenly things? No one has ascended into heaven except the one who descended from heaven, the Son of Man. And just as Moses lifted up the serpent in the wilderness, so must the Son of Man be lifted up, that whoever believes in him may have eternal life.

"For God so loved the world that he gave his only Son, so that everyone who believes in him may not perish but may have eternal life.

"Indeed, God did not send the Son into the world to condemn the world but in order that the world might be saved through him.

-John 3:1–17

Through the Mystical Lens

We ask the questions together with our ancestors, "How can I be born anew?" "How is Spirit inviting us to move as One?"

In the "now-stories" of Abram's blessing and Nicodomus's inquiry, an alluring voice calls us into deeper layers of surrender-trust, beyond the certainty-craving mind. We are asked to drop out of the anxious grasp of the known, and fall—groundless—into the open Heart of mystery, where there is no bottom to reach and no top to contain. This is to be reborn of Spirit, again and again: allowing Spirit to breathe us, a new creation, moment by moment, awakened to emptiness that is full, and fullness that is empty—a spaciousness that always welcomes More.

To be born from above—the wind, the spirit, the breath (πνεῦμα)—all move where they will. Spirit stirs life in unexpected places. To consent: "Yes, you may." Even if Spirit carries us where our hearts and minds are reluctant to go, the invitation remains.

Relax, ask, listen, move: alive within this present stream. We are not alone, rowing gently within and with our dreams, aware of a Presence more Real than the passing fears of drowning. Taking refuge in the breath—in the deep, slow Spirit, breathed in and breathed out —we find ourselves kissed by mystery and beauty of all of Creation, blessed and blessing, in Spirit's embrace.

-Rev. Brent Reynolds, Vine Contemplative Community + Tribe of the Open Heart

Reflection Questions

1. Brent writes of "allowing Spirit to breathe us, a new creation, moment by moment." When have you experienced yourself being breathed by something greater rather than doing the breathing?
2. The reflection speaks of consenting to Spirit even when it "carries us where our hearts and minds are reluctant to go." What resistance have you encountered when invited into spiritual rebirth, and how did you move through it?
3. "A spaciousness that always welcomes More." How do you experience the relationship between emptiness and fullness in your spiritual life? When has letting go created more room for the sacred?

Spiritual Practice for the Week

This week, practice being "breathed by Spirit" through conscious surrender:

Find a comfortable position and begin noticing your natural breath. Don't control it; simply observe. After a few minutes, shift your awareness: instead of "I am breathing," sense "I am being breathed."

With each inhale, silently say: "Spirit breathes me in." With each exhale: "Spirit breathes me out."

When your mind insists on taking control of the breath, gently return to being breathed. Notice any anxiety about letting go of control. This is the "anxious grasp of the known" that Brent describes.

Practice for 10 minutes daily. As you become comfortable, carry this awareness into daily activities. Walking: "I am being walked." Speaking: "I am being spoken through." Notice how this shift from doing to being done through opens you to the movement of Spirit.

Journal Prompts

Nicodemus came to Jesus "by night," under cover of darkness, perhaps hiding from colleagues or his own doubts. Write about a time when you sought spiritual truth in secret or in the margins of your regular life. What did the darkness provide that daylight couldn't?

The reflection invites us to fall "groundless, into the open Heart of mystery, where there is no bottom to reach and no top to contain." Describe an experience of spiritual groundlessness that initially felt threatening but ultimately revealed itself as freedom. What had to die for this spaciousness to be born?

LENT 3: THE SAMARITAN WOMAN AT THE WELL

The Reading

So he came to a Samaritan city called Sychar, near the plot of ground that Jacob had given to his son Joseph. Jacob's well was there, and Jesus, tired out by his journey, was sitting by the well. It was about noon.

A Samaritan woman came to draw water, and Jesus said to her, "Give me a drink." (His disciples had gone to the city to buy food.) The Samaritan woman said to him, "How is it that you, a Jew, ask a drink of me, a woman of Samaria?" (Jews do not share things in common with Samaritans.) Jesus answered her, "If you knew the gift of God and who it is that is saying to you, 'Give me a drink,' you would have asked him, and he would have given you living water." The woman said to him, "Sir, you have no bucket, and the well is deep. Where do you get that living water? Are you greater than our ancestor Jacob, who gave us the well and with his sons and his flocks drank from it?" Jesus said to her, "Everyone who drinks of this water will be thirsty again, but those who drink of the water that I will give them will never be thirsty. The water that I will give will become in them a spring of water gushing up to eternal life." The woman said to him, "Sir, give me this water, so that I may never be thirsty or have to keep coming here to draw water."

Many Samaritans from that city believed in him because of the woman's testimony, "He told me everything I have ever done." So when the Samaritans came to him, they asked him to stay with them, and he stayed there two days. And many more believed because of his word. They said to the woman, "It is no longer because of what you said that we believe, for we have heard for ourselves, and we know that this is truly the Savior of the world."

-John 4:5-15, 39-42

Through the Mystical Lens

Some moments come to us like noon in the desert — bright, unsheltered, revealing more than we're ready to face. That's where we meet the Samaritan woman: alone at the well, carrying a story that didn't fit inside polite religion.

Tradition has often framed her as "morally questionable," but the text never says that. More likely, she was the kind of person life had tossed around. Loss, abandonment, maybe tragedy. She keeps going, keeps surviving. But she's learned to make her daily pilgrimage alone.

Many of us know that feeling — the quiet walk to a place we don't want others to see.

And then she meets Jesus.

He doesn't shield His eyes from the glare of her noonday truth. He doesn't ask her to fix anything first.

He simply says, "Give me a drink."

A divine request from a tired stranger.

A God who begins from vulnerability, not power.

Sometimes, in prayer or expanded awareness, we meet the One who does the same with us — not accusing, but inviting. Not performing a miracle on our wounds, but sitting with us beside them. Asking us to participate. Offering relationship before answers.

As their conversation unfolds, He speaks of "living water"— something that rises from within. Not poured on us from outside, but awakened inside. A spring that doesn't run dry.

Some of us have tasted that — in worship, in silence, under stars, or in moments of consciousness so wide we learned that the Holy was not far away, but within us.

As close as breath.

As steady as a well beneath cracked ground.

Jesus names her story without shame. And something shifts. The one who avoided her neighbors runs to them. The one who felt disqualified becomes a witness. The one who hid at noon becomes a source of revelation.

In her awakening, the whole village is transformed.

Maybe that's the path:

Not escaping our story, but letting it be seen in the light.

Trusting that the Holy meets us there — not with judgment, but with living water.

Today, may you find Christ already sitting beside your well at noon, whispering:

"There's a spring within you. Let's draw from it together."

-Rev. Dr. Andrea F. Smith, United Methodist

Reflection Questions

1. Andrea writes of moments that come "like noon in the desert —bright, unsheltered, revealing more than we're ready to face." When has spiritual light exposed parts of your story you'd rather keep hidden, and how did that exposure become liberation?
2. The reflection describes Jesus as "not performing a miracle on our wounds, but sitting with us beside them." How does this differ from what you've expected from the divine? When has presence been more healing than fixing?
3. The woman who "avoided her neighbors runs to them" after encountering living water within. What inner spring, once discovered, has compelled you to share what you previously hid?

Spiritual Practice for the Week

This week, practice "Meeting at the Well":

Each day at noon (or another consistent time), pause wherever you are. This is your well: the place where you meet both your thirst and the Source.

Sit quietly and ask: "What am I thirsting for today?" Don't judge what arises: longing for rest, meaning, connection, escape. Simply acknowledge the thirst.

Then place your hand on your heart and breathe deeply. With each breath, imagine a spring of living water within you: something already there, waiting to be uncapped.

Ask: "What if what I'm seeking is already within me?"

Spend five minutes simply feeling for that inner spring. You might sense it as warmth, spaciousness, quiet joy, or simple presence. Trust whatever you find.

Before returning to your day, offer one small act of vulnerability: a text of appreciation, an honest conversation, a creative expression, letting your inner water flow outward.

Journal Prompts

The woman at the well made her "daily pilgrimage alone," avoiding others. Write about a part of your spiritual journey you've kept hidden or separate from your community. What would it mean to bring this into the light, to let it become part of your witness?

Jesus says the living water will become "a spring...gushing up to eternal life" from within. Describe a time when you discovered an inner resource you didn't know you had, perhaps during crisis, in deep meditation, or through plant medicine. How did finding this inner spring change your relationship to external sources of validation or fulfillment?

LENT 4: JESUS HEALS A MAN BORN BLIND

The Reading

A Man Born Blind Receives Sight

As he walked along, he saw a man blind from birth. His disciples asked him, "Rabbi, who sinned, this man or his parents, that he was born blind?" Jesus answered, "Neither this man nor his parents sinned; he was born blind so that God's works might be revealed in him. We must work the works of him who sent me while it is day; night is coming, when no one can work. As long as I am in the world, I am the light of the world." When he had said this, he spat on the ground and made mud with the saliva and spread the mud on the man's eyes, saying to him, "Go, wash in the pool of Siloam" (which means Sent). Then he went and washed and came back able to see. The neighbors and those who had seen him before as a beggar began to ask, "Is this not the man who used to sit and beg?" Some were saying, "It is he." Others were saying, "No, but it is someone like him." He kept saying, "I am he." But they kept asking him, "Then how were your eyes opened?" He answered, "The man called Jesus made mud, spread it on my eyes, and said to me, 'Go to Siloam and wash.' Then I went and washed and received my sight." They said to him, "Where is he?" He said, "I do not know."

The Pharisees Investigate the Healing

They brought to the Pharisees the man who had formerly been blind. Now it was a Sabbath day when Jesus made the mud and opened his eyes. Then the Pharisees also began to ask him how he had received his sight. He said to them, "He put mud on my eyes. Then I washed, and now I see." Some of the Pharisees said, "This man is not from God, for he does not observe the Sabbath." Others said, "How can a man who is a sinner perform such signs?" And they were divided. So they said again to the blind man, "What do you say about him? It was your eyes he opened." He said, "He is a prophet."

The Jews did not believe that he had been blind and had received his sight until they called the parents of the man who had received his sight and asked them, "Is this your son, who you say was born blind? How then does he now see?" His parents answered, "We know that this is our son and that he was born blind, but we do not know how it is that now he sees, nor do we know who opened his eyes. Ask him; he is of age. He will speak for himself." His parents said this because they were afraid of the Jews, for the Jews had already agreed that anyone who confessed Jesus to be the Messiah would be put out of the synagogue. Therefore his parents said, "He is of age; ask him."

So for the second time they called the man who had been blind, and they said to him, "Give glory to God! We know that this man is a sinner." He answered, "I do not know whether he is a sinner. One thing I do know, that though I was blind, now I see." They said to him, "What did he do to you? How did he open your eyes?" He answered them, "I have told you already, and you would not listen. Why do you want to hear it again?

Do you also want to become his disciples?" Then they reviled him, saying, "You are his disciple, but we are disciples of Moses. We know that God has spoken to Moses, but as for this man, we do not know where he comes from." The man answered, "Here is an astonishing thing! You do not know where he comes from, yet he opened my eyes. We know that God does not listen to sinners, but he does listen to one who worships him and obeys his will. Never since the world began has it been heard that anyone opened the eyes of a person born blind. If this man were not from God, he could do nothing." They answered him, "You were born entirely in sins, and are you trying to teach us?" And they drove him out.

Spiritual Blindness

Jesus heard that they had driven him out, and when he found him he said, "Do you believe in the Son of Man?" He answered, "And who is he, sir? Tell me, so that I may believe in him." Jesus said to him, "You have seen him, and the one speaking with you is he." He said, "Lord, I believe." And he worshiped him. Jesus said, "I came into this world for judgment, so that those who do not see may see and those who do see may become blind." Some of the Pharisees who were with him heard this and said to him, "Surely we are not blind, are we?" Jesus said to them, "If you were blind, you would not have sin. But now that you say, 'We see,' your sin remains.

-John 9:1–41

Through the Mystical Lens

"Who sinned," the disciples asked. "Who messed up? Somebody's wrong, right?"

"Isn't that the guy who used to sit and beg," the neighbors asked. "We recognize him. He was one of those people."

"We're not blind are we," the Pharisees asked. "You're not saying we've got issues, are you?"

Labels. Finger pointing. Accusations. "Oh, they're the problem," we say. "That type of person in the White House creates a mess. People who go to those churches don't understand the gospel as clearly as we do."

Self righteousness. Segregation. Oppression. "I'm more enlightened than you are," we might not say out loud, but maybe we think smugly to ourselves. "Those neighbors are driving down my property values. People who vote that way are wrong; they're the problem."

The 13th century Persian poet Rumi said this about labels, judgment, and sin:

> *Out beyond ideas of wrongdoing and rightdoing,*
> *There is a field. I'll meet you there.*
> *When the soul lies down in that grass,*
> *The world is too full to talk about.*
> *Ideas, language, even the phrase each other*
> *Doesn't make any sense.*[1]

Imagine this: The man born blind, the neighbors, the disciples, and Jesus splayed out in a field, bare feet with toes scratching the fertile soil, heads lolled on the gently breathing chests of another, mouths empty of words that don't make sense, hearts too full of love to talk about, souls resting in the grass and full of Spirit.

Or, imagine this: The man born blind diving into the Pool of Siloam with the skill of Olympian Tom Daley. And all around him the

---

1. Translated from Persian by Coleman Barks and John Moyne, from *The Essential Rumi,* published by HarperCollins. Copyright © 1995 by Coleman Barks.

disciples splashing in the water, wearing those elaborate feathered swim caps like Esther Williams in "Million Dollar Mermaid." Alongside them, a gaggle of Pharisees bobbing about in yellow duckie innertubes. Neighbors serving hot dogs and potato salad. And Jesus, in cheap sunglasses, floating on a raft, cueing up a pool party playlist that starts with One Republic's "I Ain't Worried" that merges into Katrina and The Waves' "Walking on Sunshine."

Imagine.

-Rev. Dr. Timothy Tutt, United Church of Christ

Reflection Questions

1. The reflection invites us to imagine everyone lying in Rumi's field "beyond rightdoing and wrongdoing." When have you experienced this dissolution of judgment in expanded consciousness? How do you return to a world of necessary distinctions while holding that unity awareness?
2. The pool party image transforms a miraculous healing into joyful celebration. After your own spiritual "sight" has opened, how do you balance the seriousness of transformation with the playfulness of divine comedy? What helps you avoid becoming a "Pharisee in a duckie innertube"?
3. "I am the man," the healed one insists when others doubt his transformation. When others question whether you're still the same person after spiritual awakening, how do you affirm both continuity and radical change? What gives you courage to claim your new sight?

Spiritual Practice for the Week

Each morning this week, practice "fresh sight meditation." Begin with eyes closed, sitting in darkness like the man born blind. Rest here for 5 minutes, noticing what arises when physical sight is absent.

Then slowly open your eyes as if seeing for the first time. Look at familiar objects and people with the wonder of new sight. Throughout your day, when you catch yourself seeing through old labels and judgments, close your eyes briefly and reopen them. Ask: "What would I see if I had no history with this person/situation?"

In the spirit of the pool party imagery, let this practice be playful. You're learning to see anew, like someone adjusting to sight after blindness. Be patient with yourself as you practice dropping the labels that obscure clear seeing.

Journal Prompts

The reflection moves from finger-pointing ("Who sinned?") to Rumi's field beyond all judgment. Write about a time when your own spiritual opening dissolved your need to assign blame. What replaced that old way of organizing reality? How do you navigate a world that still operates on fault-finding?

"Imagine," the reflection ends, inviting us into playful sacred imagery. Create your own imaginative scene where a moment from your spiritual journey becomes a celebration. Who's there? What music plays? How does reimagining your transformation as joyful rather than serious shift something in you?

LENT 5: THE RAISING OF LAZARUS

The Reading

The Death of Lazarus

Now a certain man was ill, Lazarus of Bethany, the village of Mary and her sister Martha. Mary was the one who anointed the Lord with perfume and wiped his feet with her hair; her brother Lazarus was ill. So the sisters sent a message to Jesus, "Lord, he whom you love is ill." But when Jesus heard it, he said, "This illness does not lead to death; rather, it is for God's glory, so that the Son of God may be glorified through it." Accordingly, though Jesus loved Martha and her sister and Lazarus, after having heard that Lazarus was ill, he stayed two days longer in the place where he was.

Then after this he said to the disciples, "Let us go to Judea again." The disciples said to him, "Rabbi, the Jews were just now trying to stone you, and are you going there again?" Jesus answered, "Are there not twelve hours of daylight? Those who walk during the day do not stumble because they see the light of this world. But those who walk at night stumble because the light is not in them." After saying this, he told them, "Our friend Lazarus has fallen asleep, but I am going there to awaken him." The disciples said to him, "Lord, if he has fallen asleep, he will be all right." Jesus, however, had been speaking about his death, but they thought that he was referring merely to sleep. Then Jesus told them plainly, "Lazarus is dead. For your sake I am glad I was not there, so that you may believe. But let us go to him." Thomas, who was called the Twin, said to his fellow disciples, "Let us also go, that we may die with him."

Jesus the Resurrection and the Life

When Jesus arrived, he found that Lazarus had already been in the tomb four days. Now Bethany was near Jerusalem, some two miles away, and many of the Jews had come to Martha and Mary to console them about their brother. When Martha heard that Jesus was coming, she went and met him, while Mary stayed at home. Martha said to Jesus, "Lord, if you had been here, my brother would not have died. But even now I know that God will give you whatever you ask of him." Jesus said to her, "Your brother will rise again." Martha said to him, "I know that he will rise again in the resurrection on the last day." Jesus said to her, "I am the resurrection and the life. Those who believe in me, even though they die, will live, and everyone who lives and believes in me will never die. Do you believe this?" She said to him, "Yes, Lord, I believe that you are the Messiah, the Son of God, the one coming into the world."

Jesus Weeps

When she had said this, she went back and called her sister Mary and told her privately, "The Teacher is here and is calling for you." And when she heard it, she got up quickly and went to him. Now Jesus had not yet come to the village but was still at the place where Martha had met him. The

Jews who were with her in the house consoling her saw Mary get up quickly and go out. They followed her because they thought that she was going to the tomb to weep there. When Mary came where Jesus was and saw him, she knelt at his feet and said to him, "Lord, if you had been here, my brother would not have died." When Jesus saw her weeping and the Jews who came with her also weeping, he was greatly disturbed in spirit and deeply moved. He said, "Where have you laid him?" They said to him, "Lord, come and see." Jesus began to weep. So the Jews said, "See how he loved him!" But some of them said, "Could not he who opened the eyes of the blind man have kept this man from dying?"

Jesus Raises Lazarus to Life
Then Jesus, again greatly disturbed, came to the tomb. It was a cave, and a stone was lying against it. Jesus said, "Take away the stone." Martha, the sister of the dead man, said to him, "Lord, already there is a stench because he has been dead four days." Jesus said to her, "Did I not tell you that if you believed you would see the glory of God?" So they took away the stone. And Jesus looked upward and said, "Father, I thank you for having heard me. I knew that you always hear me, but I have said this for the sake of the crowd standing here, so that they may believe that you sent me." When he had said this, he cried with a loud voice, "Lazarus, come out!" The dead man came out, his hands and feet bound with strips of cloth and his face wrapped in a cloth. Jesus said to them, "Unbind him, and let him go."

The Plot to Kill Jesus
Many of the Jews, therefore, who had come with Mary and had seen what Jesus did believed in him.

-John 11:1-45

Through the Mystical Lens

Ever since I began working as a chaplain in pediatric healthcare, I've wrestled with the Lazarus story. People often read it as proof that miracles, including raising the dead can happen if your faith is strong enough. Too often I've encountered parents and families grieving over the loss of a child and they ask, "Why didn't God do anything?" I've been asked that question or something like it many, many times. Here we see God reversing death and many of us are left asking, "Why not my loved one?"

The Gospel writer makes certain we know Lazarus wasn't just "mostly dead." He was four days gone. Sealed in a tomb. Decomposing. There is no physiological loophole: he had *fully died.* And when Jesus arrives he doesn't stride in triumphantly, confident in the miracle he is about to perform. He weeps. Scripture says he was *deeply disturbed* (*embrimáomai*) a word for a grief so physical the body convulses with it. This is not gentle sadness. It is sorrow that strikes at his core along with fear, anger, and hopelessness. In our mystical encounter, these emotions can feel more pronounced or distant, overwhelming or powerless. Our experience of them can be just as revealing as their presence.

Before there is a resurrection, there is a Christ who *is broken by grief.*

For me, that is the part that matters most in the story: Jesus does not avoid grief by reversing death. He does not experience human sorrow from a distance. Christ is *undone* by it, like many of us have been.

The more I sit with this story, the more I am convinced it is less about the miracle of resurrection and more about the power of grief. Grief moves us. Grief changes us. Grief can cause the very Son of God to weep. Any one of us, if we had the power, would raise from the dead someone we loved. I often think that's because we don't want to feel alone in the midst of grief, which is often one of the loneliest moments we can experience.

LENT 5: THE RAISING OF LAZARUS

Sometimes the miracle is not what gets resurrected.

Sometimes the miracle is that we are not left alone.

God knows grief, too.

-Rev. B. Jeffrey Vidt, United Church of Christ

Reflection Questions

1. Jeffrey asks about "encounters with grief" that remain unsettled. What loss in your life still carries unresolved questions? How might sitting with the mystery be its own form of healing?
2. The reflection shifts focus from resurrection as reversal to presence in grief. When has someone's willingness to be "undone" by your pain meant more than their attempts to fix it?
3. "God knows grief, too." How does imagining the divine as intimately acquainted with loss change your relationship to your own sorrow?

Spiritual Practice for the Week

This week, practice "Holding Death and Resurrection":

Find a quiet space and settle into a comfortable position. Hold your hands in front of you, palms up.

In your left hand, imagine holding death: loss, grief, endings. In your right, hold resurrection: new life, hope, transformation. Feel the weight of both.

Notice any tendency to drop one or reach for the other. When you feel pulled toward resurrection, gently return to holding both. When grief feels too heavy, resist the urge to escape; simply breathe.

As you hold this paradox, remember Jeffrey's insight: "Sometimes the miracle is not what gets resurrected. Sometimes the miracle is that we are not left alone." The presence holding both death and resurrection with you; this may be the truest miracle.

Pay attention to:

- Physical sensations as you balance these realities
- Emotions that arise from holding paradox
- Memories that surface
- Any spiritual tilting toward one or the other

End by bringing your hands together at your heart, acknowledging that both death and resurrection live within you, and that you are not alone in holding them.

Journal Prompts

Jeffrey writes that "Before there is a resurrection, there is a Christ who is broken by grief." Describe a time when you witnessed someone powerful or divine being undone by human sorrow. How did their vulnerability change your understanding of strength?

"Sometimes the miracle is not what gets resurrected. Sometimes the miracle is that we are not left alone." Write about a loss where the hoped-for reversal didn't come. What presence appeared instead? How was that its own form of resurrection?

PASSION SUNDAY (PALM SUNDAY): THE PASSION ACCORDING TO MATTHEW

The Reading

Jesus's Triumphal Entry into Jerusalem

When they had come near Jerusalem and had reached Bethphage, at the Mount of Olives, Jesus sent two disciples, saying to them, "Go into the village ahead of you, and immediately you will find a donkey tied and a colt with her; untie them and bring them to me. If anyone says anything to you, just say this, 'The Lord needs them.' And he will send them immediately." This took place to fulfill what had been spoken through the prophet:

"Tell the daughter of Zion,
Look, your king is coming to you,
humble and mounted on a donkey,
and on a colt, the foal of a donkey."

The disciples went and did as Jesus had directed them; they brought the donkey and the colt and put their cloaks on them, and he sat on them. A very large crowd spread their cloaks on the road, and others cut branches from the trees and spread them on the road. The crowds that went ahead of him and that followed were shouting,

"Hosanna to the Son of David!

Blessed is the one who comes in the name of the Lord!

Hosanna in the highest heaven!"

When he entered Jerusalem, the whole city was in turmoil, asking, "Who is this?" The crowds were saying, "This is the prophet Jesus from Nazareth in Galilee."

-Matthew 21:1–11

Pilate Questions Jesus

Now Jesus stood before the governor, and the governor asked him, "Are you the king of the Jews?" Jesus said, "You say so." But when he was accused by the chief priests and elders, he did not answer. Then Pilate said to him, "Do you not hear how many accusations they make against you?" But he gave him no answer, not even to a single charge, so that the governor was greatly amazed.

Barabbas or Jesus?

Now at the festival the governor was accustomed to release a prisoner for the crowd, anyone whom they wanted. At that time they had a notorious prisoner called Jesus Barabbas. So after they had gathered, Pilate said to them, "Whom do you want me to release for you, Jesus Barabbas or Jesus who is called the Messiah?" For he realized that it was out of jealousy that they had handed him over. While he was sitting on the judgment seat, his wife sent word to him, "Have nothing to do with that innocent man, for today I have suffered a great deal because of a dream about him." Now the chief priests and the elders persuaded the crowds to ask for Barabbas and to have Jesus killed. The governor again said to them, "Which of the two do you want me to release for you?" And they said, "Barabbas." Pilate said to them, "Then what should I do with

Jesus who is called the Messiah?" All of them said, "Let him be crucified!" Then he asked, "Why, what evil has he done?" But they shouted all the more, "Let him be crucified!"

Pilate Hands Jesus Over to Be Crucified
So when Pilate saw that he could do nothing but rather that a riot was beginning, he took some water and washed his hands before the crowd, saying, "I am innocent of this man's blood; see to it yourselves." Then the people as a whole answered, "His blood be on us and on our children!" So he released Barabbas for them, and after flogging Jesus he handed him over to be crucified.

The Soldiers Mock Jesus
Then the soldiers of the governor took Jesus into the governor's headquarters, and they gathered the whole cohort around him. They stripped him and put a scarlet robe on him, and after twisting some thorns into a crown they put it on his head. They put a reed in his right hand and knelt before him and mocked him, saying, "Hail, King of the Jews!" They spat on him and took the reed and struck him on the head. After mocking him, they stripped him of the robe and put his own clothes on him. Then they led him away to crucify him.

The Crucifixion of Jesus
As they went out, they came upon a man from Cyrene named Simon; they compelled this man to carry his cross. And when they came to a place called Golgotha (which means Place of a Skull), they offered him wine to drink, mixed with gall, but when he tasted it, he would not drink it. And when they had crucified him, they divided his clothes among themselves by casting lots; then they sat down there and kept watch over him. Over his head they put the charge against him, which read, "This is Jesus, the King of the Jews."

Then two rebels were crucified with him, one on his right

and one on his left. Those who passed by derided him, shaking their heads and saying, "You who would destroy the temple and build it in three days, save yourself! If you are the Son of God, come down from the cross." In the same way the chief priests also, along with the scribes and elders, were mocking him, saying, "He saved others; he cannot save himself. He is the King of Israel; let him come down from the cross now, and we will believe in him. He trusts in God; let God deliver him now, if he wants to, for he said, 'I am God's Son.' " The rebels who were crucified with him also taunted him in the same way.

The Death of Jesus
From noon on, darkness came over the whole land until three in the afternoon. And about three o'clock Jesus cried with a loud voice, "Eli, Eli, lema sabachthani?" that is, "My God, my God, why have you forsaken me?" When some of the bystanders heard it, they said, "This man is calling for Elijah." At once one of them ran and got a sponge, filled it with sour wine, put it on a stick, and gave it to him to drink. But the others said, "Wait, let us see whether Elijah will come to save him." Then Jesus cried again with a loud voice and breathed his last. At that moment the curtain of the temple was torn in two, from top to bottom. The earth shook, and the rocks were split. The tombs also were opened, and many bodies of the saints who had fallen asleep were raised. After his resurrection they came out of the tombs and entered the holy city and appeared to many. Now when the centurion and those with him, who were keeping watch over Jesus, saw the earthquake and what took place, they were terrified and said, "Truly this man was God's Son!"

-Matthew 27:11–54

Through the Mystical Lens

The crucifixion of Jesus is a challenging and powerful story of loss. As Christ dies on the cross, a heaviness descends upon the early Christian community, and all hope seems lost.

Mystical and entheogenic experiences are not always positive, transportive, inspirational, and uplifting. Entheogenic experiences can be frightening and open pathways to our awareness of suffering and loss. Hopelessness may even descend after an entheogenic journey, like a heaviness and a dark night of the soul. Learning to make space for hopelessness and the presence of death is part of navigating spiritually transformative experiences, and having the support of a skilled companion can ease challenging experiences.

As we know from the Christian story, death is not the end, but a pathway toward a new, emergent reality. Awareness of death cannot be bypassed or skipped over, and sometimes challenging spiritual experiences may be necessary for spiritual growth and development. Whether or not they are necessary, losses are an inevitable aspect of life that cannot be avoided by anyone born into a human body. In an entheogenic healing experience, I once received the message, "it is what it is" in response to tragic suffering in my own life. Loss "is what it is", but loss is not the end of the story for Christians who affirm the healing presence of love even in the direst of circumstances.

Entheogens and deep spiritual practices can open awareness to suffering—our own suffering and the reality of suffering around us. If we seek to flee this awareness, it can grow even stronger and more fearful. Accepting suffering with a loving determination to align with our highest values can allow for a softening of fear and hopelessness.

-Jamie Beachy, MDiv, PhD, Mennonite

Reflection Questions

1. Jamie asks how love serves as a resource for facing suffering in deep spiritual experiences. When has love, not as feeling but as commitment, sustained you through a dark night of the soul?
2. The reflection mentions receiving the message "it is what it is" about tragic suffering. How do you hold both acceptance of what cannot be changed and active engagement with what can be transformed?
3. "How does loss sometimes create the possibility for transformation?" Reflect on a loss that seemed only destructive at the time but later revealed itself as clearing space for new life.

Spiritual Practice for the Week

This week, practice "Honoring Loss with Living Values":

Create a simple altar or designate a space on your desk. Place there:

1. An object representing a current loss or suffering (personal or collective): perhaps a photo, a small stone, or a written word
2. Beside it, place something symbolizing one of your highest values: a candle for hope, a feather for freedom, a seed for growth

Each day, spend five minutes with these objects. Don't try to fix or spiritually bypass the loss. Simply hold both realities: "This suffering is real" and "This value still lives in me."

Notice how your chosen value might guide your response to the suffering. Not to eliminate it, but to meet it with integrity.

At week's end, consider: How does affirming your values in the face of loss change your relationship to both?

Journal Prompts

The reflection mentions receiving the message "it is what it is" in response to tragic suffering. Write about a time when you received a simple but profound message during a difficult experience. How did this message help you accept what couldn't be changed while still engaging with what could be transformed?

Jamie notes that "challenging spiritual experiences may be necessary for spiritual growth." Describe an experience, whether in ceremony, crisis, or daily life, where difficulty became teacher. How did you learn to stay present with what wanted to flee?

HOLY WEEK

MAUNDY THURSDAY: THE LAST SUPPER AND THE NEW COMMANDMENT

The Reading

Jesus Washes the Disciples' Feet

Now before the festival of the Passover, Jesus knew that his hour had come to depart from this world and go to the Father. Having loved his own who were in the world, he loved them to the end. The devil had already decided that Judas son of Simon Iscariot would betray Jesus. And during supper Jesus, knowing that the Father had given all things into his hands and that he had come from God and was going to God, got up from supper, took off his outer robe, and tied a towel around himself. Then he poured water into a basin and began to wash the disciples' feet and to wipe them with the towel that was tied around him. He came to Simon Peter, who said to him, "Lord, are you going to wash my feet?" Jesus answered, "You do not know now what I am doing, but later you will understand." Peter said to him, "You will never wash my feet." Jesus answered, "Unless I wash you, you have no share with me." Simon Peter said to him, "Lord, not my feet only but also my hands and my head!" Jesus said to him, "One who has bathed does not need to wash, except for the feet, but is entirely clean. And you are clean, though not all of you." For he knew who was to betray him; for this reason he said, "Not all of you are clean."

After he had washed their feet, had put on his robe, and had reclined again, he said to them, "Do you know what I have done to you? You call me Teacher and Lord, and you are right, for that is what I am. So if I, your Lord and Teacher, have washed your feet, you also ought to wash one another's feet. For I have set you an example, that you also should do as I have done to you. Very truly, I tell you, slaves are not greater than their master, nor are messengers greater than the one who sent them. If you know these things, you are blessed if you do them.

The New Commandment
When he had gone out, Jesus said, "Now the Son of Man has been glorified, and God has been glorified in him. If God has been glorified in him, God will also glorify him in himself and will glorify him at once. Little children, I am with you only a little longer. You will look for me, and as I said to the Jews so now I say to you, 'Where I am going, you cannot come.' I give you a new commandment, that you love one another. Just as I have loved you, you also should love one another. By this everyone will know that you are my disciples, if you have love for one another."

-John 13:1–17, 31–35

Through the Mystical Lens

As New Testament scholar Jaime Clark-Soles points out in her book "Reading John for Dear Life: A Spiritual Walk through the Fourth Gospel," (p. 87) the 13th chapter of John's gospel begins and ends in love. John tells us who Jesus is when he writes, "Having loved his own who were in the world, he loved them to the end." And Jaime's response to this verse is, "Indeed. Did then and does now." Jesus loves - to the end of the story, to the end of our stories.

Recent explorations in the use of psychedelics with end-of-life care patients demonstrates that these medicines have much to teach us in the ways of death and dying. This is Jesus' farewell discourse in John's gospel. He anticipates the horrors yet to come, and what does he choose to do? Wash feet. Comfort his anxious friends. Teach about love.

During my first ever psilocybin journey in a clinical study at Johns Hopkins, I encountered my own death by experiencing it as if I were Jesus dying into the arms of his mother, Mary. The tableau in my mind mirrored Michaelangelo's great sculpture, "La Pieta." As I lay dying, I saw my guides in the room as angels, and knew tremendous peace and love, even as I viscerally knew Mary's sadness at the same time. Now, I don't know if the peace I made with death that day will endure for the rest of my days, but I can say with assurance forevermore that I believe our stories begin and end in love.

John gives us an amazing glimpse into this room where a mystical experience of the love of Christ happens. The love of Christ washes us clean, sanctifies us, and calls us to love one another with the depth of compassion Christ has shown to us. Then, Jesus tells his disciples that it is their love for one another that will make their devotion to Christ known in the world. Christ's consistent command never changes, never hesitates, never adds additional terms or conditions. It is always "Love one another." And, it's as simple - and as difficult - as that.

-Rev. Kerra Becker English, Presbyterian

Reflection Questions

1. Kerra writes that she believes "our stories begin and end in love." Reflect on a moment when you glimpsed this truth: perhaps in deep meditation, during a journey, or at a bedside. What shifted in you?
2. Jesus washed feet knowing Judas would betray him, yet loved him anyway. When have you been called to offer tender service to someone who might wound you? How did this vulnerability transform you?
3. The reflection connects Jesus's farewell acts with end-of-life wisdom. What has death (literal or ego death) taught you about what matters most? How do you carry that wisdom forward?

Spiritual Practice for the Week

This week, practice "Gazing with Christ's Eyes":

Partner with someone you trust: a friend, family member, or spiritual companion. Sit facing each other in comfortable silence.

Set a timer for 5 minutes. Simply look into each other's eyes without speaking. When discomfort arises (giggling, looking away, tears), gently return to gazing.

See if you can look at this person the way Jesus looked at his disciples: knowing their flaws, their fears, their coming betrayals and denials, and loving them completely anyway.

After 5 minutes, bow to each other in recognition of the holy you've witnessed.

If you're alone, practice this with your own reflection, offering yourself the same unconditional gaze Christ offers you.

End by washing your hands mindfully, feeling the water as blessing, remembering that love flows through the simplest acts of care.

Journal Prompts

Kerra describes experiencing her death as Jesus dying in Mary's arms, feeling both "tremendous peace and love" and Mary's sadness simultaneously. Write about a time when you held multiple truths at once: joy and sorrow, death and life, ending and beginning. How did this paradox reveal something about love's nature?

Julian of Norwich wrote that no creature can know "how sweetly and how tenderly our Creator loves us." Spend time imagining you could fully feel this tender love for just one minute. What would change in how you see yourself? What burdens would you set down? What forgiveness would flow?

GOOD FRIDAY: THE PASSION ACCORDING TO JOHN

The Reading

The Betrayal and Arrest of Jesus

After Jesus had spoken these words, he went out with his disciples across the Kidron Valley to a place where there was a garden, which he and his disciples entered. Now Judas, who betrayed him, also knew the place because Jesus often met there with his disciples. So Judas brought a detachment of soldiers together with police from the chief priests and the Pharisees, and they came there with lanterns and torches and weapons. Then Jesus, knowing all that was to happen to him, came forward and asked them, "Whom are you looking for?" They answered, "Jesus of Nazareth." Jesus replied, "I am he." Judas, who betrayed him, was standing with them. When Jesus said to them, "I am he," they stepped back and fell to the ground. Again he asked them, "Whom are you looking for?" And they said, "Jesus of Nazareth." Jesus answered, "I told you that I am he. So if you are looking for me, let these people go." This was to fulfill the word that he had spoken, "I did not

lose a single one of those whom you gave me." Then Simon
Peter, who had a sword, drew it, struck the high priest's slave,
and cut off his right ear. The slave's name was Malchus. Jesus
said to Peter, "Put your sword back into its sheath. Am I not to
drink the cup that the Father has given me?"

Jesus before the High Priest
So the soldiers, their officer, and the Jewish police arrested
Jesus and bound him. First they took him to Annas, who was
the father-in-law of Caiaphas, the high priest that year.
Caiaphas was the one who had advised the Jews that it was
better to have one person die for the people.

Peter Denies Jesus
Simon Peter and another disciple followed Jesus. Since that
disciple was known to the high priest, he went with Jesus into
the courtyard of the high priest, but Peter was standing
outside at the gate. So the other disciple, who was known to
the high priest, went out, spoke to the woman who guarded
the gate, and brought Peter in. The woman said to Peter, "You
are not also one of this man's disciples, are you?" He said, "I
am not." Now the slaves and the police had made a charcoal
fire because it was cold, and they were standing around it and
warming themselves. Peter also was standing with them and
warming himself.

The High Priest Questions Jesus
Then the high priest questioned Jesus about his disciples and
about his teaching. Jesus answered, "I have spoken openly to
the world; I have always taught in synagogues and in the
temple, where all the Jews come together. I have said nothing
in secret. Why do you ask me? Ask those who heard what I
said to them; they know what I said." When he had said this,
one of the police standing nearby struck Jesus on the face,
saying, "Is that how you answer the high priest?" Jesus

answered, "If I have spoken wrongly, testify to the wrong. But if I have spoken rightly, why do you strike me?" Then Annas sent him bound to Caiaphas the high priest.

Peter Denies Jesus Again

Now Simon Peter was standing and warming himself. They asked him, "You are not also one of his disciples, are you?" He denied it and said, "I am not." One of the slaves of the high priest, a relative of the man whose ear Peter had cut off, asked, "Did I not see you in the garden with him?" Again Peter denied it, and at that moment the cock crowed.

Jesus before Pilate

Then they took Jesus from Caiaphas to Pilate's headquarters. It was early in the morning. They themselves did not enter the headquarters, so as to avoid ritual defilement and to be able to eat the Passover. So Pilate went out to them and said, "What accusation do you bring against this man?" They answered, "If this man were not a criminal, we would not have handed him over to you." Pilate said to them, "Take him yourselves and judge him according to your law." The Jews replied, "We are not permitted to put anyone to death." (This was to fulfill what Jesus had said when he indicated the kind of death he was to die.)

Then Pilate entered the headquarters again, summoned Jesus, and asked him, "Are you the King of the Jews?" Jesus answered, "Do you ask this on your own, or did others tell you about me?" Pilate replied, "I am not a Jew, am I? Your own nation and the chief priests have handed you over to me. What have you done?" Jesus answered, "My kingdom does not belong to this world. If my kingdom belonged to this world, my followers would be fighting to keep me from being handed over to the Jews. But as it is, my kingdom is not from here." Pilate asked him, "So you are a king?" Jesus answered, "You say that I am a king. For this I was born, and for this I came into the world, to testify to the truth. Everyone who belongs to the truth listens to my voice." Pilate asked him, "What is truth?"

Jesus Sentenced to Death

After he had said this, he went out to the Jews again and told them, "I find no case against him. But you have a custom that I release someone for you at the Passover. Do you want me to release for you the King of the Jews?" They shouted in reply, "Not this man but Barabbas!" Now Barabbas was a rebel.

Then Pilate took Jesus and had him flogged. And the soldiers wove a crown of thorns and put it on his head, and they dressed him in a purple robe. They kept coming up to him, saying, "Hail, King of the Jews!" and striking him on the face. Pilate went out again and said to them, "Look, I am bringing him out to you to let you know that I find no case against him." So Jesus came out wearing the crown of thorns and the purple robe. Pilate said to them, "Behold the man!" When the chief priests and the police saw him, they shouted, "Crucify him! Crucify him!" Pilate said to them, "Take him yourselves and crucify him; I find no case against him." The Jews answered him, "We have a law, and according to that law he ought to die because he has claimed to be the Son of God."

Now when Pilate heard this, he was more afraid than ever. He entered his headquarters again and asked Jesus, "Where are you from?" But Jesus gave him no answer. Pilate therefore said to him, "Do you refuse to speak to me? Do you not know that I have power to release you and power to crucify you?" Jesus answered him, "You would have no power over me unless it had been given you from above; therefore the one who handed me over to you is guilty of a greater sin." From then on Pilate tried to release him, but the Jews cried out, "If you release this man, you are no friend of Caesar. Everyone who claims to be a king sets himself against Caesar."

When Pilate heard these words, he brought Jesus outside and sat on the judge's bench at a place called The Stone Pavement, or in Hebrew Gabbatha. Now it was the day of Preparation for the Passover, and it was about noon. He said to the Jews, "Here is your King!" They cried out, "Away with him! Away with him! Crucify him!" Pilate asked them, "Shall I crucify your King?" The chief priests answered, "We have no king but Caesar." Then he handed him over to them to be crucified.

The Crucifixion of Jesus

So they took Jesus, and carrying the cross by himself he went out to what is called the Place of the Skull, which in Hebrew is called Golgotha. There they crucified him and with him two others, one on either side, with Jesus between them. Pilate also had an inscription written and put on the cross. It read, "Jesus of Nazareth, the King of the Jews." Many of the Jews read this inscription because the place where Jesus was crucified was near the city, and it was written in Hebrew, in Latin, and in Greek. Then the chief priests of the Jews said to Pilate, "Do not write, 'The King of the Jews,' but, 'This man said, I am King of the Jews.' " Pilate answered, "What I have written I have written." When the soldiers had crucified Jesus, they took his clothes and divided them into four parts, one for each soldier. They also took his tunic; now the tunic was seamless, woven in one piece from the top. So they said to one another, "Let us not tear it but cast lots for it to see who will get it." This was to fulfill what the scripture says,

"They divided my clothes among themselves,
    and for my clothing they cast lots."

And that is what the soldiers did.

Meanwhile, standing near the cross of Jesus were his mother, and his mother's sister, Mary the wife of Clopas, and Mary Magdalene. When Jesus saw his mother and the disciple whom he loved standing beside her, he said to his mother,

"Woman, here is your son." Then he said to the disciple, "Here is your mother." And from that hour the disciple took her into his own home.

After this, when Jesus knew that all was now finished, he said (in order to fulfill the scripture), "I am thirsty." A jar full of sour wine was standing there. So they put a sponge full of the wine on a branch of hyssop and held it to his mouth. When Jesus had received the wine, he said, "It is finished." Then he bowed his head and gave up his spirit.

Jesus's Side Is Pierced

Since it was the day of Preparation, the Jews did not want the bodies left on the cross during the Sabbath, especially because that Sabbath was a day of great solemnity. So they asked Pilate to have the legs of the crucified men broken and the bodies removed. Then the soldiers came and broke the legs of the first and of the other who had been crucified with him. But when they came to Jesus and saw that he was already dead, they did not break his legs. Instead, one of the soldiers pierced his side with a spear, and at once blood and water came out. (He who saw this has testified so that you also may continue to believe. His testimony is true, and he knows that he tells the truth.) These things occurred so that the scripture might be fulfilled, "None of his bones shall be broken." And again another passage of scripture says, "They will look on the one whom they have pierced."

The Burial of Jesus

After these things, Joseph of Arimathea, who was a disciple of Jesus, though a secret one because of his fear of the Jews, asked Pilate to let him take away the body of Jesus. Pilate gave him permission, so he came and removed his body. Nicodemus, who had at first come to Jesus by night, also came, bringing a mixture of myrrh and aloes, weighing about a hundred pounds. They took the body of Jesus and wrapped it with the spices in linen cloths, according to the burial custom of the Jews. Now there was a garden in the place where he was crucified, and in the garden there was a new tomb in which no one had ever been laid. And so, because it was the Jewish day of Preparation and the tomb was nearby, they laid Jesus there.

-John 18:1 – 19:42

Through the Mystical Lens

The striking juxtaposition of characters in this Passion narrative invites the wondering question that Pilate names explicitly, "What is truth?" In the realm of the mystical path, each tradition moves us toward the unitive understanding of what is True. Pilate is clearly searching, as are the disciples, especially Judas and Peter. The priests, the crowds, the officials are also responding out of their inner division. Compare their words and actions with that of the three Mary's, Joseph, Nicodemus, and of course Jesus. Their collective unitive posture in this passage is striking when you place them alongside the uncertainty and divided characters.

When we step into this narrative ourselves, the divided/unitive binary we see is that some of us are questioning reality and some of us are in a unitive state with reality. Reality in this sense is that which is true. What is also true is that most of us live, most of the time, between the binaries, vacillating to and fro.

My own journey within the spectrum of the divided/unitive binary is fraught with a lot of uncertainty and doubt, and quite a lot of grief. Finding my ground in the unitive state has been evasive at best. I'm more like Pilate and act more like Judas and Peter than I care to admit.

My first experience with psilocybin medicine came at a time when I was grieving the loss of my father. In my grief I felt divided within myself and split from Creator and Spirit. I struggled to remember who I truly was. Like Judas I was betraying God. Like Peter I was denying the One I made vows to follow. Because like Pilate I could no longer discern what was true. The medicine was like surgery for my soul and brought me back to myself. Under that surgical darkness I slipped into the Truth: all is One and that One is Love Divine. My split self dissolved as my true self re-emerged as one with God. I awoke whole and could face my reality like those who remained resilient and resolved to his death and burial, maybe even trusting death is not a final separation, rather a step toward something more true.

-The Rev. Cn. Jonathan E. Myers, Priest in the Episcopal Church

Reflection Questions

1. Jonathan identifies with Pilate's question "What is truth?" and admits to acting "more like Judas and Peter than I care to admit." Which character in the Passion narrative most reflects your own spiritual struggles, and what does this recognition teach you?
2. The reflection contrasts the "divided" characters (Pilate, Judas, Peter) with the "unitive" ones (the three Marys, Jesus). When have you experienced this shift from inner division to unitive awareness, and what facilitated that movement?
3. Jonathan describes his grief creating a split from Creator and Spirit. How has loss or trauma affected your sense of connection to the divine, and what has helped restore wholeness?

Spiritual Practice for the Week

This week, practice "Standing at the Cross" meditation:

Each day, spend 10 minutes with one character from the Passion narrative. Monday: Pilate. Tuesday: Peter. Wednesday: Judas. Thursday: Mary Magdalene. Friday: Jesus.

Sit quietly and embody their perspective. Feel their confusion, fear, grief, or surrender. Don't judge—simply inhabit their experience.

Notice where you feel divided within yourself as you hold their story. Where do you feel unified? What splits you from your truth? What returns you to wholeness?

On Saturday, rest in silence, holding all these perspectives simultaneously. Feel how division and unity coexist in the human experience.

On Sunday, place your hand on your heart and affirm: "All is One and that One is Love Divine." Feel any split parts of yourself gently gathering into wholeness.

Journal Prompts

Jonathan writes that psilocybin helped him slip "into the Truth: all is One and that One is Love Divine." Describe a moment when you touched this unitive awareness: whether through medicine, meditation, or crisis. How did experiencing this Truth change your relationship to the divisions and betrayals within yourself?

The reflection suggests that "death is not a final separation, rather a step toward something more true." Write about a death (literal, ego, relationship, identity) that initially felt like ultimate division but revealed itself as a doorway to greater unity. What had to be trusted for this revelation to emerge?

HOLY SATURDAY: THE SPACE BETWEEN

The Reading

The Burial of Jesus

When it was evening, there came a rich man from Arimathea named Joseph, who also was himself a disciple of Jesus. He went to Pilate and asked for the body of Jesus; then Pilate ordered it to be given to him. So Joseph took the body and wrapped it in a clean linen cloth and laid it in his new tomb, which he had hewn in the rock. He then rolled a great stone to the door of the tomb and went away. Mary Magdalene and the other Mary were there, sitting opposite the tomb.

The Guard at the Tomb

The next day, that is, after the day of Preparation, the chief priests and the Pharisees gathered before Pilate and said, "Sir, we remember what that impostor said while he was still alive, 'After three days I will rise again.' Therefore command the tomb to be made secure until the third day; otherwise, his disciples may go and steal him away and tell the people, 'He has been raised from the dead,' and the last deception would be worse than the first." Pilate said to them, "You have a guard of soldiers; go, make it as secure as you can." So they went with the guard and made the tomb secure by sealing the stone.

-Matthew 27:57-66

Through the Mystical Lens

Well, this is pretty much the prototypical psychedelic text! After a trauma, a person takes a psychedelic medicine, goes into an enclosed place to explore what no one else can see, has a trip sitter or two, while fear and protectors show up to do their jobs.

But the deeper invitation of Holy Saturday is not about modeling a psychedelic experience.

The Church almost always ignores this day in the church calendar. Usually it's the day for volunteers to hurriedly put away the remnants of Good Friday services and prepare the church for a blowout Great Vigil or huge Easter celebration. It's a flurry of filling the church with fragrant white lilies, polishing the silver, setting up a new Paschal candle, ironing the fanciest linens and vestments, and confirming the extra paid trumpet player. In my Catholic school upbringing, it was the day you did your spring cleaning to "get ready" for the coming of Christ. Not bad, but I think it still missed the point by literally sweeping away the mess and message of waiting in the dark through unresolved times.

What if we held Holy Saturday as the day that honors the terrain in which most of our lives are lived? The reality of the long journey between being wounded and healed? The endless yearning for love and union, the bottomless pit of grief and loss, the unresolved pain, or the ongoing presence of fear? Holy Saturday is the site of what remains after trauma; the dark deadness of waiting for light to return, meaning to be made, and hope to be restored. How often does trauma get transformed in a day or over a weekend or even in a single psychedelic journey? If we let it, Holy Saturday models for us the most honest reality of where we spend much of our lives, the holding of mystery, and the slow work of integration.

Like the Marys outside the tomb, Holy Saturday teaches us how to witness loss without trying to fix it, to patiently offer compassion to the horrible, the hidden, and the hurt. Knowing that Jesus didn't come into the fullness of his Christ-ness until he'd spent time in the in-between, we can trust that any unknown territory we're willing to explore in prayer or therapy or even in safe psychedelic experiences is the landscape Christ knows and inhabits, waiting there to meet us.

-The Rev. Wendy D. Cliff, Episcopal

Reflection Questions

1. Wendy describes Holy Saturday as "the long journey between being wounded and healed." What unresolved territory are you currently inhabiting? How might honoring this in-between space, rather than rushing toward resolution, be its own form of spiritual practice?
2. The reflection asks: "How often does trauma get transformed in a day or over a weekend or even in a single psychedelic journey?" Reflect on your own expectations versus reality about healing timelines. Where have you learned patience with the slow work of integration?
3. Like the Marys sitting outside the tomb, we're called to "witness loss without trying to fix it." When have you been able to offer this quality of presence to your own pain or another's? What makes this witnessing different from passive resignation?

Spiritual Practice for the Week

This week, practice "Holy Saturday Vigil: Keeping Watch in the In-Between":

Each morning, identify one area of your life that exists in Holy Saturday territory: the space between wound and healing, loss and renewal, death and resurrection.

Set aside 10 minutes to practice what the Marys modeled outside the tomb. Sit quietly with this unresolved place in your life. Don't prepare for Easter or try to hurry the resurrection. Simply keep vigil.

As you sit, breathe slowly and repeat: "I honor this in-between space. This too is sacred ground." Notice any discomfort with the unfinished, any urge to rush toward resolution or "spring clean" the messiness away.

When impatience arises, return to Wendy's wisdom: most of life is lived in this terrain. Place your hand on your heart and offer yourself the same patient presence the Marys offered at the tomb: witnessing without fixing, accompanying without answers.

Close by remembering: "Christ knows this landscape of waiting. I am not alone in the slow work of integration."

Journal Prompts

Wendy writes about churches hurrying to "literally sweep away the mess and message of waiting in the dark." Explore a time when you or others tried to rush you through grief, trauma, or difficulty toward premature resurrection. What was lost in that rushing? What might have been gained by honoring the full duration of your Holy Saturday?

Holy Saturday reveals that "any unknown territory we're willing to explore...is the landscape Christ knows and inhabits, waiting there to meet us." Describe an experience of meeting the sacred precisely in the unresolved, the liminal, or the incomplete. How did this encounter differ from meeting the divine in moments of clarity or resolution?

EASTER

EASTER DAY: THE RESURRECTION AND THE EMPTY TOMB

The Reading

The Resurrection of Jesus

Early on the first day of the week, while it was still dark, Mary Magdalene came to the tomb and saw that the stone had been removed from the tomb. So she ran and went to Simon Peter and the other disciple, the one whom Jesus loved, and said to them, "They have taken the Lord out of the tomb, and we do not know where they have laid him." Then Peter and the other disciple set out and went toward the tomb. The two were running together, but the other disciple outran Peter and reached the tomb first. He bent down to look in and saw the linen wrappings lying there, but he did not go in. Then Simon Peter came, following him, and went into the tomb. He saw the linen wrappings lying there, and the cloth that had been on Jesus's head, not lying with the linen wrappings but rolled up in a place by itself. Then the other disciple, who reached the tomb first, also went in, and he saw and believed, for as yet they did not understand the scripture, that he must rise from the dead. Then the disciples returned to their homes.

Jesus Appears to Mary Magdalene

But Mary stood weeping outside the tomb. As she wept, she bent over to look into the tomb, and she saw two angels in white sitting where the body of Jesus had been lying, one at the head and the other at the feet. They said to her, "Woman, why are you weeping?" She said to them, "They have taken away my Lord, and I do not know where they have laid him." When she had said this, she turned around and saw Jesus standing there, but she did not know that it was Jesus. Jesus said to her, "Woman, why are you weeping? Whom are you looking for?" Supposing him to be the gardener, she said to him, "Sir, if you have carried him away, tell me where you have laid him, and I will take him away." Jesus said to her, "Mary!" She turned and said to him in Hebrew, "Rabbouni!" (which means Teacher). Jesus said to her, "Do not touch me, because I have not yet ascended to the Father. But go to my brothers and say to them, 'I am ascending to my Father and your Father, to my God and your God.' " Mary Magdalene went and announced to the disciples, "I have seen the Lord," and she told them that he had said these things to her.

-John 20:1–18

Through the Mystical Lens

Jesus asked, "Woman, why are you weeping? Who are you looking for?" in response to Mary Magdalene's tears and distress. Isn't that how we often enter a medicine journey? We take the step to enter a journey, assuming we will find the answer to a burning question in one way and the answer comes from a completely different direction! Mary went to the tomb expecting to find the body of her Lord and Savior, Jesus. When she found the empty tomb, she told others and they came to see as well. The others took what they saw at assumed face value and left. For some reason, however, Mary remained and looked again into the darkness of the tomb. As she did, she had a truly mystical experience. Her assumptions and understanding of life and death were obliterated.

Psychedelic journeys offer this gift as well. By looking into the darkness, at our greatest fears, questions, and sorrows, and staying with them, we may find our greatest treasures and wisdom, available directly to us in a lived experience beyond all logical explanation. They teach that this material world is not all there is to experience. We may experience a dissolution of the ego, a "dying before we die". We may come face to face with our own mortality but also be assured of our soul's immortality as well. Mary experienced a truly ineffable experience as she dared to wait at the tomb, look into the darkness, ask her soul's deepest questions, and stay - even in heartbreak. Her answer came from an unexpected direction and completely expanded her understanding of what she thought was possible.

The medicine does similar work - shining a light on truths we cannot see with our natural eyesight and in our logical reasoning, but truth that has been there all along. We are eternal beings. Death is temporary. Resurrection is possible. And darkness may be the birth canal for our most amazing miracles and deepest wisdom. And, like Mary, we will never be the same.

-Jan Owen, LPC and Baptist Minister

Reflection Questions

1. Jan writes, "We take the step to enter a journey, assuming we will find the answer to a burning question in one way and the answer comes from a completely different direction!" When have your own mystical or medicine experiences surprised

you with answers you weren't seeking? How did receiving unexpected wisdom change your original questions?

2. "The others took what they saw at assumed face value and left. For some reason, however, Mary remained." After a powerful spiritual experience, how do you discern when to move on versus when to stay present with mystery? What has remaining in uncertainty taught you that quick answers never could?

3. Jan suggests "darkness may be the birth canal for our most amazing miracles and deepest wisdom." How has your willingness to face darkness in expanded states transformed your relationship with difficult emotions or life circumstances? What continues to be born from these encounters?

Spiritual Practice for the Week

Each morning this week, practice "staying at the tomb" as Mary did. Set aside 15 minutes to sit with one question or area of grief in your life. Rather than seeking immediate answers or resolution, simply be present with the darkness.

Begin by naming what feels lost or uncertain. Then, like Mary looking into the empty tomb, gently turn your attention toward the darkness itself. What does this emptiness feel like in your body? What arises when you stop trying to fix or understand?

After 10 minutes of sitting with the question, ask softly: "What wants to be revealed here?" Listen without forcing. Sometimes, like Mary, you may hear your name called from an unexpected direction. Other times, the gift may simply be your increased capacity to be present with mystery.

Journal Prompts

Jan describes Mary's experience: "Her assumptions and understanding of life and death were obliterated." Write about a moment in your own journey when everything you thought you knew dissolved. What assumptions died? What understanding emerged from that obliteration? How do you live differently now?

"We may come face to face with our own mortality but also be assured of our soul's immortality as well." Explore a time when you experienced both your finite nature and your eternal essence simultaneously. How do you hold these seeming opposites? What wisdom emerged from touching both death and deathlessness?

EASTER 2: THE RISEN CHRIST APPEARS TO THOMAS

The Reading

Jesus Appears to the Disciples

When it was evening on that day, the first day of the week, and the doors were locked where the disciples were, for fear of the Jews, Jesus came and stood among them and said, "Peace be with you." After he said this, he showed them his hands and his side. Then the disciples rejoiced when they saw the Lord. Jesus said to them again, "Peace be with you. As the Father has sent me, so I send you." When he had said this, he breathed on them and said to them, "Receive the Holy Spirit. If you forgive the sins of any, they are forgiven them; if you retain the sins of any, they are retained."

Jesus and Thomas

But Thomas (who was called the Twin), one of the twelve, was not with them when Jesus came. So the other disciples told him, "We have seen the Lord." But he said to them, "Unless I see the mark of the nails in his hands and put my finger in the mark of the nails and my hand in his side, I will not believe."

A week later his disciples were again in the house, and Thomas was with them. Although the doors were shut, Jesus came and stood among them and said, "Peace be with you." Then he said to Thomas, "Put your finger here and see my hands. Reach out your hand and put it in my side. Do not doubt but believe." Thomas answered him, "My Lord and my God!" Jesus said to him, "Have you believed because you have seen me? Blessed are those who have not seen and yet have come to believe."

The Purpose of This Book
Now Jesus did many other signs in the presence of his disciples that are not written in this book. But these are written so that you may continue to believe that Jesus is the Messiah, the Son of God, and that through believing you may have life in his name.

-John 20:19–31

Through the Mystical Lens

I was ordained on December 21, 2004, which in the Christian calendar is the Feast of St. Thomas. A welcome synchronicity, Thomas's experience aligned very well with my spirituality as well as my journey toward ordination. Experiences of the Holy had been a regular occurrence throughout my life, sometimes in church, but just as often when I was able to quiet my mind and body or when I was out in nature. In my early 30s, I began discerning ordination to help others have experiences of God.

Before seminary and the deeper dive into scripture that those 3 years offered me, I had held the conventional view of this post-resurrection appearance of Jesus and the reaction of "Doubting Thomas".

Something like, "poor Thomas, if only he had been more faithful, he would not have needed the 'proof' that touching the wounds gave him."

While I have always known that God is present and active in the world and in my own life, there have been many times that I needed a spiritual booster shot, not unlike Thomas in this story. Twelve years into my ordained ministry, felt experiences of God had largely been subsumed into the never-ending work of church growth and institutional maintenance. By the time I had the good fortune to be a 2016 participant in a psilocybin study at Johns Hopkins University, I was burned out and dealing with nearly debilitating anxiety and low-grade depression.

In the first of two sessions, I had a physical and embodied awareness of the Spirit moving up my spine. The second session, a month later, opened me to the deeply prayerful experience of my ordination being renewed and expanded. Over the next weeks, the anxiety and depression lifted, and I had renewed clarity about and commitment to my vocation and new vision of the power of the Spirit.

Thomas was a follower of Jesus willing to ask questions that others were afraid to ask. "Honest Thomas" or "Seeking Thomas" invites us to see questioning and the longing for authentic experience as vital components of spiritual growth, not as evidence of spiritual Failure.

-Hunt Priest, M.Div. Former Episcopal priest.

Reflection Questions

1. Hunt reframes Thomas as "Honest Thomas" or "Seeking Thomas" rather than "Doubting Thomas." When have your spiritual questions or need for direct experience been misunderstood as lack of faith? How did you find validation for your seeking?

2. The reflection describes needing a "spiritual booster shot" after twelve years of ministry. What sustains your faith between peak experiences? When have you needed to touch the wounds, to have direct contact with the sacred, to renew your belief?

3. Hunt's psilocybin experience brought "renewed clarity about and commitment to my vocation." How do mystical experiences reshape not just what we believe, but how we serve? What expanded vision have you received?

Spiritual Practice for the Week

This week, practice "Sacred Questioning":

Each day, identify one spiritual belief or practice you've accepted without direct experience. Hold it gently, like Thomas held his need to touch the wounds.

Ask yourself: What would direct experience of this truth feel like in my body? Where am I settling for secondhand faith when I long for firsthand encounter? What "proof" does my soul legitimately need?

Rather than judging your questions, honor them as Hunt honors Thomas as "vital components of spiritual growth." Notice where you've been taught that questioning equals spiritual failure.

If you have access to contemplative practices, psychedelics, or time in nature, use these as opportunities to seek the "spiritual booster shot" your soul might need. Trust that your longing for authentic experience is holy.

Journal Prompts

Hunt describes the Spirit moving up his spine in his first psilocybin session, followed by his ordination being "renewed and expanded." Write about a time when a mystical experience didn't just comfort you but commissioned you, giving you not just peace but purpose. How did it change your understanding of your calling?

The reflection notes how "felt experiences of God had largely been subsumed into the never-ending work of church growth and institutional maintenance." Explore your own relationship between institutional religious life and direct spiritual experience. When have they supported each other? When have they been at odds? How do you navigate this tension?

EASTER 3: THE ROAD TO EMMAUS

The Reading

Now on that same day two of them were going to a village called Emmaus, about seven miles from Jerusalem, and talking with each other about all these things that had happened. While they were talking and discussing, Jesus himself came near and went with them, but their eyes were kept from recognizing him. And he said to them, "What are you discussing with each other while you walk along?" They stood still, looking sad. Then one of them, whose name was Cleopas, answered him, "Are you the only stranger in Jerusalem who does not know the things that have taken place there in these days?" He asked them, "What things?" They replied, "The things about Jesus of Nazareth, who was a prophet mighty in deed and word before God and all the people, and how our chief priests and leaders handed him over to be condemned to death and crucified him. But we had hoped that he was the one to redeem Israel. Yes, and besides all this, it is now the third day since these things took place. Moreover, some women of our group astounded us. They were at the tomb early this morning, and when they did not find his body there they came back and told us that they had indeed seen a vision of angels who said that he was alive. Some of those who were with us went to the tomb and found it just as the women had said, but they did not see him." Then he said to them, "Oh, how foolish you are and how slow of heart to believe all that the prophets have declared! Was it not necessary that the Messiah should suffer these things and then enter into his glory?" Then beginning with Moses and all the prophets, he interpreted to them the things about himself in all the scriptures.

As they came near the village to which they were going, he walked ahead as if he were going on. But they urged him strongly, saying, "Stay with us, because it is almost evening and the day is now nearly over." So he went in to stay with them. When he was at the table with them, he took bread, blessed and broke it, and gave it to them. Then their eyes were opened, and they recognized him, and he vanished from their sight. They said to each other, "Were not our hearts burning within us while he was talking to us on the road, while he was opening the scriptures to us?" That same hour they got up and returned to Jerusalem, and they found the eleven and their companions gathered together. They were saying, "The Lord has risen indeed, and he has appeared to Simon!" Then they told what had happened on the road and how he had been made known to them in the breaking of the bread.

-Luke 24:13–35

Through the Mystical Lens

There are moments when recognition shatters the ordinary. The Emmaus travelers model to us how a soul awakens not just in solitude but through shared pathways, traveling in conversation, and breaking bread with strangers who reveal themselves as divine.

The passage highlights the importance of companionship and mutual witnessing that is needed for our spiritual and ceremonial lives. Many of the practices that lead to altered consciousness are hyper-individualized and even when we are in group settings, we are often encouraged to stay in our own process. But this passage invites us onto a path of mutual witnessing. We are not here to ascend alone.

Like the Emmaus travelers, our soul's recognition happens in the alchemy of witness. You see the Divine in others when the walk is made together and the meal is shared.

The recognition may happen during a ceremony or during integration afterwards but it always blooms in the fire of the heart and the hunger of the soul. It may come as warmth in the chest, as a knowing in the bones, or as holy fire stirred by the presence of another. In the end, it is not the psychedelic experience that saves us but rather communion with others.

And when the Divine is recognized in company, may we say again:

"Were not our hearts burning within us?"

The Emmaus story is an embodied mystery encouraging us to journey with others and to pay close attention to what we are witnessing during an experience. It teaches us that in one instant something we are interacting with can shift into something deeper.

May we always remember: the Divine walks beside us, cloaked in mystery and unveiled in the feast.

-Dr. Jessica Felix Romero

Reflection Questions

1. Jessica writes that "it is not the psychedelic experience that saves us but rather communion with others." How has sharing your journey with trusted companions transformed experiences that might have remained incomplete if processed alone?
2. The reflection describes recognition that "may come as warmth in the chest, as a knowing in the bones, or as holy fire stirred by the presence of another." When have you experienced this embodied recognition of the Divine through witnessing or being witnessed during integration?
3. "Many of the practices that lead to altered consciousness are hyper-individualized," Jessica observes, yet the Emmaus story shows awakening through companionship. How do you balance the need for inner work with the necessity of communal processing in your spiritual practice?

Spiritual Practice for the Week

This week, practice "Sacred Witnessing in Daily Life."

Each day, choose one ordinary activity to share with another person: a meal, a walk, a conversation over tea. As you engage, hold the awareness that Christ may be present in disguise. Notice moments when the ordinary shifts into something deeper. Pay attention to warmth in your chest, sudden insights, or the feeling of holy ground beneath ordinary conversation.

After each shared experience, take five minutes alone to journal: What did I witness in the other person? What might they have witnessed in me? Were there moments when "our hearts were burning within us"?

At week's end, if comfortable, share with your companion what you noticed during your time together. You might discover that what seemed ordinary to you was transformative for them, or vice versa.

Journal Prompts

Jessica describes how "the Divine walks beside us, cloaked in mystery and unveiled in the feast." Write about a time when someone you thought was just a fellow traveler revealed themselves as a bearer of divine wisdom or healing. What was the moment of unveiling? How did sharing a meal or journey together create the conditions for recognition?

"You see the Divine in others when the walk is made together and the meal is shared." Reflect on an integration circle, ceremony, or spiritual gathering where collective witnessing revealed something you couldn't have seen alone. What emerged in the space between you and others that wouldn't have appeared in solitary practice?

EASTER 4: THE GOOD SHEPHERD

The Reading

"Very truly, I tell you, anyone who does not enter the sheepfold by the gate but climbs in by another way is a thief and a bandit. The one who enters by the gate is the shepherd of the sheep. The gatekeeper opens the gate for him, and the sheep hear his voice. He calls his own sheep by name and leads them out. When he has brought out all his own, he goes ahead of them, and the sheep follow him because they know his voice. They will not follow a stranger, but they will run from him because they do not know the voice of strangers." Jesus used this figure of speech with them, but they did not understand what he was saying to them.

So again Jesus said to them, "Very truly, I tell you, I am the gate for the sheep. All who came before me are thieves and bandits, but the sheep did not listen to them. I am the gate. Whoever enters by me will be saved and will come in and go out and find pasture. The thief comes only to steal and kill and destroy. I came that they may have life and have it abundantly.

-John 10:1-10

Through the Mystical Lens

John's Gospel delights in mixed metaphors. Jesus is both shepherd and gate—the one who leads and the passage itself. The gate is not a wall or a checkpoint but an opening, an invitation to enter life fully. Resurrection tears down every barrier—between God and creation, self and other, life and death.

I think of barriers being removed whenever I approach my soul work with psychedelics. I strive to use them reverently and with intention. In my striving, I discover that these substances unveil what the Gospel declares: that love is the deepest reality and that separation is an illusion. Psychedelics do not replace faith or the sacraments, but they can illuminate them—revealing how the Kingdom of God is not somewhere else, but right here, shimmering beneath the surface of things, around, between, and within us.

In these sacred moments, the self expands beyond its small boundaries. The heart opens. The mind perceives the world as infused with meaning, connection, and light. These are experiences of grace—temporary, but profoundly instructive. They point toward what Jesus calls "life abundant." The same love that raised Christ from the dead is the force that dissolves fear and shame, restoring us to unity with all life.

Yet revelation is never the end of the story. The real work begins afterward: integrating the vision into daily life. The Gospel gate stands open not for escape, but for transformation. Each act of compassion, justice, and creativity becomes a way of walking through that gate once more.

Whether in prayer, in Eucharist, or in a moment of awe on a psychedelic journey, Christ the Gate invites us to awaken to the truth already within and around us: that God's love permeates all creation.

To step through this gate is to live as resurrected people—free, connected, and alive to the abundance of God's world.

-The Rev. Dr. Paul D. Fromberg, Episcopal Church

Reflection Questions

1. Paul writes that "revelation is never the end of the story. The real work begins afterward: integrating the vision into daily life." What vision or insight from your spiritual journey still seeks integration? Where is the gap between what you've seen and how you live?
2. The reflection describes Jesus as "both shepherd and gate—the one who leads and the passage itself." When have you experienced the divine as both guide and gateway? How does this paradox reshape your understanding of spiritual authority?
3. Paul states that psychedelics "unveil what the Gospel declares: that love is the deepest reality and that separation is an illusion." How do you maintain this awareness of unity when the ordinary world insists on separation? What helps you remember that division is the illusion?

Spiritual Practice for the Week

This week, practice "Walking Through the Open Gate":

Each morning, visualize yourself standing before an open gate. This is the Christ-Gate Paul describes: an invitation into abundant life. Breathe deeply and notice: What hesitation arises? What calls you forward?

Throughout your day, practice recognizing gates rather than walls. When you encounter a difficult person, situation, or emotion, pause and ask: "Where is the opening here? How might this be a passage rather than an obstacle?"

Before any act of service, creativity, or compassion, touch your heart and acknowledge: "I am walking through the gate." Feel how each loving action is both following the shepherd's voice and passing through the opening Christ provides.

Each evening, reflect: Where did I recognize open gates today? Where did I see only walls? Remember: the gate remains open, always inviting you into "life abundant."

Journal Prompts

Paul writes of "barriers being removed" in soul work with psychedelics. Describe a time when a barrier you thought was permanent (between you and God, you and others, or parts of yourself) suddenly revealed itself as an open gate. What dissolved? What connected? How do you keep that passage open?

The reflection mentions how "Each act of compassion, justice, and creativity becomes a way of walking through that gate once more." Write about a small, daily action that has become sacred passage for you. How does this ordinary act become a threshold into abundant life? What changes when you approach it as walking through Christ's gate?

EASTER 5: JESUS THE WAY TO THE FATHER

The Reading

"Do not let your hearts be troubled. Believe in God; believe also in me. In my Father's house there are many dwelling places. If it were not so, would I have told you that I go to prepare a place for you? And if I go and prepare a place for you, I will come again and will take you to myself, so that where I am, there you may be also. And you know the way to the place where I am going." Thomas said to him, "Lord, we do not know where you are going. How can we know the way?" Jesus said to him, "I am the way and the truth and the life. No one comes to the Father except through me. If you know me, you will know my Father also. From now on you do know him and have seen him."

Philip said to him, "Lord, show us the Father, and we will be satisfied." Jesus said to him, "Have I been with you all this time, Philip, and you still do not know me? Whoever has seen me has seen the Father. How can you say, 'Show us the Father'? Do you not believe that I am in the Father and the

Father is in me? The words that I say to you I do not speak on my own, but the Father who dwells in me does his works. Believe me that I am in the Father and the Father is in me, but if you do not, then believe because of the works themselves. Very truly, I tell you, the one who believes in me will also do the works that I do and, in fact, will do greater works than these, because I am going to the Father. I will do whatever you ask in my name, so that the Father may be glorified in the Son. If in my name you ask me for anything, I will do it.

-John 14:1–14

Through the Mystical Lens

It's easy to feel out of my depth as a Jesus follower in the psychedelic world. I don't have high resolution maps of consciousness like the Tibetans, or inviolable protocols to access the wisdom of a place like some Indigenous lineages. I have Jesus, the way, the truth, and the life. He is not so much a map of the cosmos as much as a reliable compass. I don't always know exactly where I stand (in life generally or in a journey specifically), but without fail, he points me back to the Father, in all times and in all places. With the cardinal directions of birth-death and repentance-forgiveness, along with endless intermediate directions like faith, hope, lament, singleness of heart, watchfulness, peace, care for my neighbor, he is a compass for a universe held together by love, for navigating the terrain of love. He reminds me that the purpose of the journey is not to go someplace else, but to arrive in myself, in my life, in all that the present moment holds. Traveling is not about escape, but arrival with the fullness of our being. We go up to the heavens, and God is there; we go down to the depths, and God is there. As it turns out, a person contains the heavens and the depths. We travel to recollect the fullness of our being in this precious life.

"You don't have to know the way, the way knows the way," sings Lindsey Scott. Such good wisdom for those moments when I'm trying to outfox the Spirit, when knowledge about Christ overrides knowing Christ. Yet, if I can be as bold as Jesus' claim to be "the way" for just a moment: We do know the way. It's dying into eternal life, it's facing the curses with love, it's treating the vulnerability of the body not as our comeuppance, but as our strength. Good reminders for hard journeys.

-The Rev. Megan Hollaway, Episcopal

Reflection Questions

1. Megan describes Jesus as "a reliable compass" rather than a detailed map. How does this distinction between compass and map change your approach to spiritual exploration? What freedom and what challenges does this create?
2. The reflection states: "We travel to recollect the fullness of our being in this precious life." When have you experienced a journey (psychedelic or otherwise) that brought you more fully into your life rather than helping you escape it?
3. "You don't have to know the way, the way knows the way." How do you discern the difference between "knowledge about Christ" and "knowing Christ" in your own spiritual practice?

Spiritual Practice for the Week

This week, practice using Christ as your compass:

Each morning, sit quietly and imagine Jesus as a compass in your heart. Notice which direction he points you toward today: an orientation rather than a destination. Perhaps toward forgiveness, toward courage, toward rest, toward service.

Throughout the day, when you feel lost or uncertain, pause and check your inner compass. Ask: "Where does Love point me in this moment?" Trust the direction more than needing to see the whole path.

Before any significant decision or interaction, take three breaths and feel for the compass needle. Sometimes it points toward death (letting go), sometimes toward birth (new beginning). Sometimes toward lament, sometimes toward joy. Honor whatever direction emerges.

Each evening, reflect: "How did I arrive more fully in my life today?" Celebrate moments when you were present rather than escaping, when you traveled inward to recollect your fullness.

Journal Prompts

Megan writes about not having "high resolution maps" like other traditions but having Jesus who points toward Love. Write about a time when you had to navigate spiritual territory without a clear map. What served as your compass? How did uncertainty become its own teacher?

The reflection reminds us that "a person contains the heavens and the depths." Explore a moment when you discovered both heaven and hell within yourself—perhaps during a journey or deep practice. How did finding God present in both places change your understanding of what it means that Jesus is "the way"?

EASTER 6: THE PROMISE OF THE ADVOCATE

The Reading

"If you love me, you will keep my commandments. And I will ask the Father, and he will give you another Advocate, to be with you forever. This is the Spirit of truth, whom the world cannot receive because it neither sees him nor knows him. You know him because he abides with you, and he will be in you.

"I will not leave you orphaned; I am coming to you. In a little while the world will no longer see me, but you will see me; because I live, you also will live. On that day you will know that I am in my Father, and you in me, and I in you. They who have my commandments and keep them are those who love me, and those who love me will be loved by my Father, and I will love them and reveal myself to them."

-John 14:15–21

Through the Mystical Lens

Do not let your mind explode as you try to understand these words from Jesus. Three times in the chapter His disciples ask Him to explain Himself, because what He says does not seem to make sense using our left-brain way of thinking. And, two times He comforts them with the words, "Do not let your hearts be troubled", but rather believe in me, and more help will be coming, for I will not abandon you.

Jesus begins and ends our reading by connecting our love for Him with keeping His commandments. The two go hand in hand. This is not a cause-and-effect relationship, that following the rules is the test to prove you love Him. Rather, loving God and others is really evidence of our desire for God and being in God. Remember, God is Love. Loving God and others is keeping His commandments.

We are united with God. Jesus tells us He is in the Father, that Jesus is also in us, and we are in Jesus. And, when the Advocate, the Spirit of Truth comes, He will be in us as well. Not only are we united with the Trinity in this way, in love, but Jesus will also continue to reveal Himself to us. The Infinite is revealing Itself to the finite! We continue to grow in God, in Love. Be blessed knowing the love we have is from God because we are in God. He has given us this love and will continue to reveal His infinite Self (love) to our finite selves as we are able to receive it. Be present in this reality. Be blessed in Love! Come Holy Spirit!

-Doug Hoover, D.Min. - Retired Presbyterian Army Chaplain

Reflection Questions

1. Doug writes that "The Infinite is revealing Itself to the finite!" When have you experienced this ongoing revelation in

prayer, nature, or expanded states of consciousness? How did your finite self receive what was being shown?

2. Jesus promises the "Spirit of truth, whom the world cannot receive, because it neither sees him nor knows him." What has helped you see and know what others might miss? How do you hold this knowing with humility?

3. The reflection describes our union with the Trinity: "He is in the Father...Jesus is also in us, and we are in Jesus." When have you directly experienced this mystical indwelling rather than just believing it intellectually?

Spiritual Practice for the Week

This week, practice sensing the Advocate's presence within:

Morning: Upon waking, before thoughts crowd in, rest in simple awareness. This awareness itself is the Spirit of truth dwelling in you. Breathe slowly and whisper: "You are in me, I am in you."

Throughout the day: Set three gentle reminders. When they sound, pause whatever you're doing and ask: "How is the Spirit of truth revealing something to me right now?" It might come through a person's words, a sensation in your body, a sudden knowing, or a shift in perception.

Evening: Before sleep, place your hand on your heart. Feel for the Advocate's presence as the deepest truth of who you are. Rest in this recognition: you are never orphaned, never alone. The infinite dwells within your finite form.

Notice how this practice changes your relationship with everyday experiences, making each moment a potential revelation.

Journal Prompts

Doug notes that Jesus's words "do not seem to make sense using our left-brain way of thinking." Describe an experience when spiritual truth came to you through non-rational knowing, perhaps through bodily sensation, synchronicity, or expanded awareness. How did you learn to trust this different way of receiving truth?

The reflection emphasizes that "loving God and others is really evidence of our desire for God and being in God." Write about a moment when love arose in you so naturally that you recognized it wasn't something you were doing, but something flowing through you from a deeper source. How did this change your understanding of commandments and spiritual practice?

EASTER 7: JESUS PRAYS FOR HIS DISCIPLES

The Reading

After Jesus had spoken these words, he looked up to heaven and said, "Father, the hour has come; glorify your Son so that the Son may glorify you, since you have given him authority over all people, to give eternal life to all whom you have given him. And this is eternal life, that they may know you, the only true God, and Jesus Christ, whom you have sent. I glorified you on earth by finishing the work that you gave me to do. So now, Father, glorify me in your own presence with the glory that I had in your presence before the world existed.

"I have made your name known to those whom you gave me from the world. They were yours, and you gave them to me, and they have kept your word. Now they know that everything you have given me is from you, for the words that you gave to me I have given to them, and they have received them and know in truth that I came from you, and they have believed that you sent me. I am asking on their behalf; I am not asking on behalf of the world but on behalf of those whom you gave me, because they are yours. All mine are yours, and yours are mine, and I have been glorified in them. And now I am no longer in the world, but they are in the world, and I am coming to you. Holy Father, protect them in your name that you have given me, so that they may be one, as we are one.

-John 17:1–11

Through the Mystical Lens

After each of my journeys during the Religious Leaders psychedelic study at Johns Hopkins, I filled out numerous questionnaires. One of them was the Mystical Experience Questionnaire (MEQ-30). My first psychedelic experience was beautiful and moving and powerful. However, as I read over the questions on the MEQ-30, I felt like I couldn't answer most of them honestly. One question was about a 'sense of unity with the divine'. Even though my Johns Hopkins experiences were mystical, neither of them had a sense of oneness with the divine. The journeys were, however, profound for me.

The Christian way often presents itself as subsuming the individual into God and Christ, melting the separated individual into the sea of unity with God. Sometimes, we quote John the Baptist and say, "I must decrease and he (Jesus) must increase" (John 3). But John the Baptist doesn't decrease at all; he becomes even more John the Baptist as the Gospels continue. John the Baptist becomes who God meant him to be.

When we get to Jesus' prayer to, with, and for the disciples in these last chapters of John, we begin to see what John the Baptist meant when he talks about decreasing, and what 'unity with God' really means. What Jesus means is that we are meant to pattern ourselves on the model that Jesus provided. The old model and pattern must decrease, and the new model and pattern must increase. And when that happens, we become more of who we are.

The more we participate in the fluid thermodynamics of the soul, the more we allow the interpenetrating experiences of God, Christ, the Holy Spirit and self to move in and through and around each other, the more we become the singular, bizarre, unique individual God truly desires us to be. "All mine are yours and yours are mine...I am not in the world; they are in the world." We are human beings in a physical world capable of profound spiritual experiences that define who we are in the eyes of God. This is what God has done for you, as an individual in God's eye. The pattern of Christ is God's gift for us to become who we truly are meant to be.

-Rev. Dr. Seth Jones, Congregational Church

Reflection Questions

1. Seth describes how becoming more unified with God made him "more of who we are" rather than less. When has spiritual surrender paradoxically led you to become more authentically yourself? How does this differ from ego dissolution?
2. The reflection mentions "the fluid thermodynamics of the soul" with God, Christ, and Spirit moving "in and through and around each other." When have you experienced this interpenetrating flow rather than rigid boundaries between human and divine?
3. Seth notes that his mystical experiences were profound despite not having "a sense of oneness with the divine." How do you understand unity with God if it doesn't mean losing your individuality? What kind of unity preserves uniqueness?

Spiritual Practice for the Week

This week, practice "Becoming More You Through Unity":

Each morning, sit quietly and feel your unique self: your particular body, your specific thoughts, your individual story. Honor this uniqueness as God's creation.

Then open your awareness to the divine presence within and around you. Instead of trying to dissolve or merge, notice how God's presence makes you more distinctly yourself. Like a plant in sunlight becomes more fully what it is meant to be.

Throughout the day, when you feel pressure to conform or diminish yourself, pause and remember: "The pattern of Christ helps me become who I truly am meant to be."

Notice the paradox: the more you open to divine flow, the more singular and unique you become. Journal briefly each evening about moments when unity with the divine enhanced rather than erased your individuality.

Journal Prompts

Seth writes that John the Baptist "becomes even more John the Baptist" as he decreases. Reflect on a time when letting go of an old pattern or ego structure didn't diminish you but revealed more of your essential self. What decreased? What increased? How did this reshape your understanding of spiritual surrender?

The reflection describes us as "human beings in a physical world capable of profound spiritual experiences that define who we are in the eyes of God." Write about a profound spiritual experience that revealed not universal sameness but your unique place in creation. How did this experience show you both your connection to all and your irreplaceable individuality?

ASCENSION DAY: JESUS IS TAKEN UP INTO HEAVEN

The Reading

Jesus Appears to His Disciples

Then he said to them, "These are my words that I spoke to you while I was still with you—that everything written about me in the law of Moses, the prophets, and the psalms must be fulfilled." Then he opened their minds to understand the scriptures, and he said to them, "Thus it is written, that the Messiah is to suffer and to rise from the dead on the third day and that repentance and forgiveness of sins is to be proclaimed in his name to all nations, beginning from Jerusalem. You are witnesses of these things. And see, I am sending upon you what my Father promised, so stay here in the city until you have been clothed with power from on high."

The Ascension of Jesus

Then he led them out as far as Bethany, and, lifting up his hands, he blessed them. While he was blessing them, he withdrew from them and was carried up into heaven. And they worshiped him and returned to Jerusalem with great joy, and they were continually in the temple blessing God.

-Luke 24:44–53

Through the Mystical Lens

One of my favorite classes in the conservative, evangelical seminary I attended was a class on Genre in the Bible. In this class, I learned to distinguish between narrative and poetic passages in the Bible. I furthermore learned that biblical narrative, especially the gospels, was written in the genre of hagiography.

Hagiography is a style of biography that is markedly different than the style of biographies written today. When we read modern biographies, we expect to read factual stories about a person's life. In Jesus' day, the lives of people were remembered with hagiography. Hagiography is a style that includes legends and myths that are meant to evoke memory of a person's essence and character more than a factual accounting of their life.

Thus, it may be useful to read and consider that narrative of Jesus' life, including the resurrection and ascension, as myth. I have sat through innumerable sermons of well meaning pastors insisting and (attempting) to scientifically prove that Jesus physically and literally rose from the dead and ascended into heaven. I found these sermons less than useful because I think they miss the point.

To think of a story as a myth is not to say the story is not true, nor a fantasy, nor make believe. Rather, a myth invites us to consider the truth in the story rather than the truth of the story.

I don't think we can 'fact-check' our way into the miracle of Easter. Did Jesus actually, physically rise from the dead and be taken up into a place in the sky called heaven? Maybe. Or maybe not.

In Aramaic, the word 'death' means to 'exist elsewhere'.

What if heaven is not just a place to die and go to, but a place to awaken and live from?

What if the resurrection and ascension of Jesus is a myth inviting us to welcome the Love he lived and taught into our hearts?

What if, as Richard Rohr says, Christ is not Jesus' last name, but the experience of full, perfect, complete Love that Jesus lived?

And what if the 'worship' of Jesus told in this myth is not the othering of the 'savior of the world', but the 'ascribing of worth' (which is the literal meaning of 'worship') to the essence and impact of Jesus' life?

So may I invite you to read this story (myth) again, letting the words read you instead of trying to read for comprehension? With curiosity and non-judgement, notice the sensations in your body as you read. Notice the sensations as you have read my reflection. And may our hearts be broken open, again, to the wonder and awe of Love that knows no bounds nor limits!

-*James Kress, M.A., D.D., Senior Minister, Unity Center for Spiritual Growth, Couer d'Alene, ID*

Reflection Questions

1. James invites us to consider "the truth in the story rather than the truth of the story." How does approaching scripture as myth revealing essence rather than fact change what you receive from it? What truths emerge when you stop fact-checking?
2. The reflection asks: "What if heaven is not just a place to die and go to, but a place to awaken and live from?" Where do you experience yourself living from heaven now? What shifts when you see it as present reality rather than future destination?

3. James suggests worship means "ascribing worth" to Jesus's essence and impact rather than othering him as distant savior. How does this reframing change your relationship to spiritual authority and your own divine nature?

Spiritual Practice for the Week

This week, practice "Living from Heaven":

Each morning, read a passage from scripture as James suggests: "letting the words read you instead of trying to read for comprehension." Notice what sensations arise in your body. What truth wants to emerge beyond literal meaning?

Throughout the day, practice experiencing heaven as a present reality. When you feel love, joy, or connection, pause and acknowledge: "I am living from heaven right now." Notice how this awareness changes your relationship to ordinary moments.

Before sleep, reflect on Jesus's ascension as myth. Instead of asking "Did it happen?" ask "What does it mean that Love ascends and fills all things?" Feel how this truth lives in your own experience.

Journal Prompts

James learned that hagiography captures "a person's essence and character more than a factual accounting of their life." Write your own brief hagiography: What myths or stories would capture your essence better than mere facts? What legends would reveal who you truly are?

The reflection proposes that Christ is "the experience of full, perfect, complete Love that Jesus lived." Describe a moment when you touched this Christ-experience yourself. How did experiencing this Love change your need for external proof or validation of spiritual truth?

PENTECOST: JESUS APPEARS TO THE DISCIPLES

The Reading

When it was evening on that day, the first day of the week, and the doors were locked where the disciples were, for fear of the Jews, Jesus came and stood among them and said, "Peace be with you." After he said this, he showed them his hands and his side. Then the disciples rejoiced when they saw the Lord. Jesus said to them again, "Peace be with you. As the Father has sent me, so I send you." When he had said this, he breathed on them and said to them, "Receive the Holy Spirit. If you forgive the sins of any, they are forgiven them; if you retain the sins of any, they are retained."

-John 20:19–23

Through the Mystical Lens

Pentecost reminds me to ask, *What doors do I lock to the world?* There is the Big "R" Reality of Life (eternal Truth) and the small "r" reality of life (temporary perceptions shaped by ego and fear). Too often, I get swept into the latter: the noise of media, the narratives of separation on social platforms, and the constant inner drama of judgment and comparison. No peace can come from that belief system!

For me, a psilocybin journey mirrors Pentecost. The medicine becomes a sacred wind that dissolves the veil of small "r" reality, restoring divine perception. It breathes through my being, reconnecting me to the Big "R" Reality that Spirit is the life within me, not outside of me. In that space, the breath of the Holy Spirit overcomes material consciousness and restores spiritual clarity. False beliefs and inner judgments begin to dissolve, and forgiveness, especially self-forgiveness, flows freely.

Pentecost, then, is not only an event in history but a metaphysical initiation that happens within. It is the moment when Divine Breath unbolts my locked room of constricted consciousness, reminding me of the vibrational shift of an Ayahuasca purge where my inner resentment is released and I am free of all that hinders peace. The breath of the Christ consciousness clears the dense vibrations associated with fear and replaces them with peace, echoing the message, *"Receive the Holy Spirit. If you forgive the sins of any, they are forgiven them; if you retain the sins of any, they are retained."*

Sins are merely errors in consciousness, mistaken beliefs in separation from God. To forgive is to purge false mental patterns that perpetuate suffering. Forgiveness clears the mind of the small "r" reality so that I can enter the Big "R" Reality. If I "retain the sins," then I hold on to fear and bind myself to that vibration and remain in spiritual bondage.

Mystical consciousness is remembering that the Spirit that Jesus breathed upon the disciples is the same Spirit breathing through me now. When I surrender to that breath, I become peace itself, an open vessel through which the Holy Spirit moves into the world.

-Rev. Dr. Cynthia Ramirez Lindenmeyer, Center for Spiritual Living

Reflection Questions

1. Cynthia distinguishes between "Big R Reality" (eternal Truth) and "small r reality" (temporary perceptions shaped by ego and fear). When have you experienced this shift from constricted perception to expanded awareness? What opened the door?

2. The reflection describes sins as "errors in consciousness, mistaken beliefs in separation from God." How does this understanding change your relationship to forgiveness, both of self and others?

3. Cynthia writes that "to retain the sins" means to "hold on to fear and bind myself to that vibration." What fears or resentments are you still retaining? What would releasing them make possible?

Spiritual Practice for the Week

This week, practice "Opening the Locked Doors":

Each morning, sit quietly and identify one "locked door" in your consciousness. This is perhaps a resentment, shame, or fear you've been holding.

Place your hand on your heart and breathe deeply. With each inhale, imagine the Holy Spirit as a gentle wind approaching this locked door. With each exhale, feel the door beginning to open.

For ten breaths, follow Cynthia's pattern:

- Inhale: "I forgive"
- Exhale: "I am forgiven"

Throughout the day, when you notice yourself contracting into "small r reality" (judgment, comparison, fear), pause and return to your breath. Ask: "What door is trying to open here?"

Each evening, reflect: Which doors opened today? Which remain locked? Remember: the same Spirit that Jesus breathed on the disciples breathes through you now.

Journal Prompts

Cynthia describes psilocybin as "a sacred wind that dissolves the veil of small 'r' reality." Write about a time when something (a substance, practice, or experience) dissolved your habitual way of seeing and revealed a larger Reality. What veils fell away? What was revealed behind them?

The reflection compares Pentecost to "an Ayahuasca purge where my inner resentment is released." Explore your own experience of spiritual purging, whether literal or metaphorical. What needed to be released for peace to enter? How did this emptying create space for the Holy Spirit to move through you?

TRINITY SUNDAY: THE COMMISSIONING OF THE DISCIPLES

The Reading

Now the eleven disciples went to Galilee, to the mountain to which Jesus had directed them. When they saw him, they worshiped him, but they doubted. And Jesus came and said to them, "All authority in heaven and on earth has been given to me. Go therefore and make disciples of all nations, baptizing them in the name of the Father and of the Son and of the Holy Spirit and teaching them to obey everything that I have commanded you. And remember, I am with you always, to the end of the age."

-Matthew 28:16–20

Through the Mystical Lens

This passage begins on a conspicuously dark note. Eleven disciples? There are twelve. Except there aren't. Judas has just hanged himself after betraying Jesus. It's just one more thing in a long succession of

You-had-to-be-there's: They've followed Jesus as he taught and preached, as he healed leprosy, demon-possession, paralysis, and blindness. They've seen him feed a crowd of 5,000 with five loaves of bread and two fish. And they've watched him walk on water and then transfigure, radiating brilliant light. And, finally, they've seen him die.

And now? They've seen him come back to life? It's not surprising that "some doubted." Perhaps you have doubts too. Perhaps when you go to a psychedelic experience, you can't even muster up the faith and presence of mind to "set an intention." All you know is that you need something, that something's not working. Or perhaps the doubt emerges as you leave a particularly illuminating experience. "Nah," it didn't really go down like that, you think to yourself. These doubts are welcome with God, and welcome in the medicine.

But this is not the whole story because, precisely in creating space for these doubts, God uses the medicine to heal. And from that place of having been healed like those in the Gospels, you are instructed to invite others into openness to God's healing, however it may come, knowing that God is with you "always, to the end of the age."

- Bryan McCarthy, Roman Catholic Church

Reflection Questions

1. Bryan notes that "some doubted" even after witnessing resurrection. When have you experienced doubt precisely in the midst of or after profound spiritual experience? How did this doubt ultimately serve your journey?

2. The reflection mentions coming to medicine when "you can't even muster up the faith and presence of mind to 'set an intention.'" How have you found healing when approaching the sacred from a place of depletion rather than clarity?

3. From "having been healed like those in the Gospels," we're called to invite others into openness. How do you share your healing experiences without preaching or pushing, but with genuine invitation?

Spiritual Practice for the Week

This week, practice "Befriending Doubt":

Each morning, honestly inventory your doubts: about God, yourself, your experiences, your path. Write down one or two without judgment. Hold them gently like worried children rather than enemies to defeat.

Throughout the day, when doubt arises, pause and say: "Welcome. What are you here to teach me?" Notice if doubt is protecting you from disappointment, keeping you grounded, or perhaps hiding fear of your own transformation.

Before sleep, recall the promise: "I am with you always, to the end of the age." This presence remains whether you believe perfectly or doubt completely. Rest in being accompanied rather than in being certain.

At week's end, review your doubts. Have any transformed? Have any revealed themselves as doorways to deeper faith? Celebrate both the doubts that dissolved and those that remain, all are welcome in God.

Journal Prompts

Bryan describes doubt emerging when we think "Nah, it didn't really go down like that" about our own profound experiences. Write about a time when you later doubted or minimized a powerful spiritual experience. What made you question what you knew to be true? How did you find your way back to honoring what happened?

The reflection moves from "having been healed" to being "instructed to invite others." Trace your own journey from receiving healing (through any means) to feeling called to share or serve. What had to happen between your personal transformation and your readiness to companion others?

SEASON AFTER PENTECOST (PROPERS)

PROPER 4 (PENTECOST 2): THE WISE AND FOOLISH BUILDERS

The Reading

Concerning Self-Deception

"Not everyone who says to me, 'Lord, Lord,' will enter the kingdom of heaven, but only the one who does the will of my Father in heaven. On that day many will say to me, 'Lord, Lord, did we not prophesy in your name, and cast out demons in your name, and do many mighty works in your name?' Then I will declare to them, 'I never knew you; go away from me, you who behave lawlessly.'

Hearers and Doers

"Everyone, then, who hears these words of mine and acts on them will be like a wise man who built his house on rock. The rain fell, the floods came, and the winds blew and beat on that house, but it did not fall because it had been founded on rock. And everyone who hears these words of mine and does not act on them will be like a foolish man who built his house on sand. The rain fell, and the floods came, and the winds blew and beat against that house, and it fell—and great was its fall!"

Now when Jesus had finished saying these words, the crowds were astounded at his teaching, for he taught them as one having authority and not as their scribes.

-Matthew 7:21–29

Through the Mystical Lens

I can probably count the times I've been truly astonished in my life on my two hands. Maybe that means I've lived an unremarkable life, but I suspect most people could say the same. In the flood of social and traditional media coverage, our brains have been rewired to find everything as amazing to the point where nothing brings us the sense of wonder that we probably should have. When everything is designed to shock us, then virtually nothing can be full of awe.

When we become so used to the same noise, we tune things out and anything and everything becomes mundane. When our spirits become numb, we struggle to feel those things that we most deeply desire and long for anymore. There are myriad reasons why this may happen from chemical imbalances to social conditioning to trauma.

The crowds listening to Jesus finish his Sermon on the Mount are astonished at his words because he spoke with authority, unlike the scribes they were used to. The very way he spoke shook them out of their slumber to a place of heart recognition. Maybe they could sense a new possibility. Maybe they were excited to hear someone challenge the status quo. Maybe they could sense God was at hand right there, right then. Whatever it was, they were having a mystical experience. They were touching something true, but could not put words to it yet.

When we glimpse or touch something of the great mystery, we are left in wonder and amazement. I think it is increasingly hard in our day to cut through the noise and hear a harmony that will move us. It is hard to see in the darkness a flicker or mystery that will spark our imagination and hope. My own journey with plant medicine in general, but with psilocybin in particular, has helped me rediscover wonder and awe as it has helped me glimpse and touch the great mystery. Today I can see it through the dark more easily. I can hear it through the noise more succinctly.

I know Christ anew and I am continually astonished.

-The Rev. Cn. Jonathan E. Myers, Priest in the Episcopal Church

Reflection Questions

1. Jonathan writes about becoming "so used to the same noise, we tune things out." What practices or experiences have helped you cut through the numbness to rediscover genuine astonishment at the sacred?
2. The crowds recognized Jesus spoke "with authority, unlike the scribes." When have you encountered teaching or presence that carried this kind of unmistakable authority? What made it different from mere information or performance?
3. The reflection describes touching "something true, but could not put words to it yet." How do you hold and integrate wordless knowing from mystical experiences before language arrives?

Spiritual Practice for the Week

This week, practice "Recovering Astonishment":

Morning: Before checking any devices or news, spend 5 minutes with something utterly ordinary: your breath, a houseplant, the texture of your sheets. Study it as if you've never encountered it before. What have you been missing?

Midday: When you notice yourself numbing out or scrolling mindlessly, stop. Ask: "What am I avoiding feeling?" Then turn toward one real thing: the sky outside your window, the taste of your food, the sensation of your feet on the ground. Let yourself be surprised by its actuality.

Evening: Recall one moment from the day when something broke through your automatic patterns: a phrase that landed differently, a glimpse of beauty, an unexpected kindness. Hold it like the crowds held Jesus's words, knowing you've touched something true even if you can't explain it yet.

End of week: Journal about what you've rediscovered. What had grown mundane that now shimmers with presence? Where is authority speaking in your life?

Journal Prompts

Jonathan shares: "I know Christ anew and I am continually astonished." Write about a spiritual truth or presence you thought you knew, only to have it revealed to you completely fresh: whether through medicine work, crisis, or grace. How did this "knowing anew" differ from your previous understanding?

The reflection describes mystical experience as "touching something true, but could not put words to it yet." Explore a wordless knowing you've carried from a profound experience. How long did it take for language to arrive? What was it like to hold truth in your body before your mind could grasp it?

PROPER 5 (PENTECOST 3): THE CALL OF MATTHEW AND MERCY OVER SACRIFICE

The Reading

The Call of Matthew

As Jesus was walking along, he saw a man called Matthew sitting at the tax-collection station, and he said to him, "Follow me." And he got up and followed him.

And as he sat at dinner in the house, many tax collectors and sinners came and were sitting with Jesus and his disciples. When the Pharisees saw this, they said to his disciples, "Why does your teacher eat with tax collectors and sinners?" But when he heard this, he said, "Those who are well have no need of a physician, but those who are sick. Go and learn what this means, 'I desire mercy, not sacrifice.' For I have not come to call the righteous but sinners."

A Girl Restored to Life and a Woman Healed

While he was saying these things to them, suddenly a leader came in and knelt before him, saying, "My daughter has just died, but come and lay your hand on her, and she will live."

And Jesus got up and followed him, with his disciples. Then suddenly a woman who had been suffering from a flow of blood for twelve years came up behind him and touched the fringe of his cloak, for she was saying to herself, "If I only touch his cloak, I will be made well." Jesus turned, and seeing her he said, "Take heart, daughter; your faith has made you well." And the woman was made well from that moment. When Jesus came to the leader's house and saw the flute players and the crowd making a commotion, he said, "Go away, for the girl is not dead but sleeping." And they laughed at him. But when the crowd had been put outside, he went in and took her by the hand, and the girl got up. And the report of this spread through all of that district.

-Matthew 9:9–13, 18–26

Through the Mystical Lens

The Call of Matthew comes in the midst of a LOT of moving parts. Calming storms, casting out demons, instructing and empowering new followers, healing the sick and raising the dead. All of this while inviting outsiders and those who have been labeled outcasts by society to pull up a chair and join his open table ministry. This is Jesus in his Flowstate.

The notion of "flowstate"or "flow" was coined by psychologist, Mihaly Csikszentmihalyi and is this idea that being in one flow is the state of operating from an absolutely dialed in or immersed and tapping into our higher states of joy, creativity and purpose. What an absolutely epic scene it must have been for Matthew to behold. Then all of a sudden, the miracle worker from Nazareth starts to walk towards the tax man and beckons him to drop his old ways and embrace the flowstate of the Creator.

This snapshot of Jesus, seemingly brushing off the religious pearl clutching because some of the folks he was welcoming were a little too rough around the edges, and serves them a riddle that might transform their orthodoxy into orthopraxy. This is perhaps the coolest version of Jesus. These flow states, where one is able to tap into the best version of ourselves and respond to the cascade of challenges and tasks before us by harnessing our concentration, inner playfulness, and creativity are moments that we should all deeply cherish. It's in that state of being that Jesus reaffirms the spirit of his Good News movement...I've come to let folks in, not keep them out.

The selection of Matthew, very likely a less than popular tax-collector, to be among the first called to be among Jesus' inner circle, sets the tone for a pattern that is unmistakable in the Gospels. Jesus is going to consistently elevate those who have experienced the darkest nights of the soul...those who have encountered his mercy and grace...and have been empowered to go and pay it forward for the next generation of outcasts. This is the Gospel Flowstate. Flowing from a place of alignment and relationship. Never forced. Never performative. All natural spirituality.

-Rev. Ruben Nuño, Church of the Living Hope, UCC

Reflection Questions

1. Ruben asks why Jesus began his ministry with "unorthodox, taboo or problematic members of society." Who in your life represents the "tax collector" that others avoid but might be ready for transformation? How might their outsider perspective be exactly what's needed?
2. The reflection distinguishes between sacrifice that's "performative or distorted" versus authentic suffering with Christ. When has your spiritual practice felt like performance? When has it flowed from genuine compassion?
3. Jesus tells the Pharisees to "go and learn what this means." What religious certainty have you been asked to unlearn in

favor of mercy? How did that shift change your spiritual flow?

Spiritual Practice for the Week

This week, practice "Gospel Flowstate":

Each day, set an intention to operate from mercy rather than sacrifice. Before your daily tasks, ask: "How can I approach this from flow rather than force?"

Throughout the day, notice when you're tempted toward performative spirituality: doing the "right" thing for appearance rather than from authentic compassion. When you catch yourself, pause and reconnect with joy.

Follow Ruben's advice: "Follow your joy" as spiritual practice. What brings you into natural, unfettered presence? Do that thing, whether it's dancing, gardening, or deep conversation, with full attention while allowing natural flow.

Each evening, reflect: Where did I flow with mercy today? Where did I get stuck in sacrificial performance? No judgment; just noticing the difference.

Journal Prompts

Ruben invites you to recall moments of flowstate when "you were in your flow" despite deadlines and stressors. Describe one such time in detail. What conditions allowed you to tap into that "higher state of joy, creativity and purpose"? How might you invite those conditions into your spiritual practice?

The reflection describes Jesus "brushing off the religious pearl clutching" to welcome rough-around-the-edges people. Write about a time when you had to choose between religious respectability and radical inclusion. What did choosing mercy over propriety cost you? What did it give you?

PROPER 6 (PENTECOST 4): THE SENDING OF THE TWELVE

The Reading

The Harvest Is Great, the Laborers Few

Then Jesus went about all the cities and villages, teaching in their synagogues and proclaiming the good news of the kingdom and curing every disease and every sickness. When he saw the crowds, he had compassion for them because they were harassed and helpless, like sheep without a shepherd. Then he said to his disciples, "The harvest is plentiful, but the laborers are few; therefore ask the Lord of the harvest to send out laborers into his harvest."

The Twelve Apostles

Then Jesus summoned his twelve disciples and gave them authority over unclean spirits, to cast them out, and to cure every disease and every sickness. These are the names of the twelve apostles: first, Simon, also known as Peter, and his brother Andrew; James son of Zebedee and his brother John; Philip and Bartholomew; Thomas and Matthew the tax collector; James son of Alphaeus and Thaddaeus; Simon the Cananaean and Judas Iscariot, the one who betrayed him.

The Mission of the Twelve
These twelve Jesus sent out with the following instructions: "Do not take a road leading to gentiles, and do not enter a Samaritan town, but go rather to the lost sheep of the house of Israel. As you go, proclaim the good news, 'The kingdom of heaven has come near.' Cure the sick; raise the dead; cleanse those with a skin disease; cast out demons. You received without payment; give without payment.

-Matthew 9:35–10:8

Through the Mystical Lens

I imagine the Sending of the Twelve. I imagine them vibrating with possibility, their hearts alive with joy and trembling with fear. To be sent out with authority—oh my gosh—how much humility that required, and at the same time, how much confidence in the One who sent them.

Once, on a flight to Israel with a group of pilgrims, I met a young woman standing outside the airplane bathroom. She was bubbling over with excitement and told me that God had sent her to Israel. She carried no purse, no provisions, not even a checkbook. All she had was the name of someone she hoped would receive her when she arrived. "God will provide," she said with radiant joy. At the time I thought, how thrilling and how incredibly naïve. Yet as I read this gospel, I am reminded of her. That kind of enthusiasm, sincerity, and even naïveté must have marked the apostles when Jesus sent them out.

I recognize something of that same spirit in my own journey with sacred medicine. Like the apostles, I want to be accompanied by wisdom, and I am deeply grateful for the science that is unfolding.

But at some point faith asks for more than research and reason—it asks for a leap. A leap into trust. A willingness to walk in Spirit.

I did not enter the medicine world casually. I went because my soul was aching, my grief was heavy, and I longed for freedom. What I discovered was healing: demons of despair loosening their grip, joy returning, a new sense of life unfolding. Just as the Twelve were sent to heal and to liberate, I, too, have seen liberation take place—in myself and in others.

Not everyone will hear this as good news, but those who are ready will recognize it. And so I imagine myself among the Twelve—fragile yet empowered, naïve perhaps, but also alive with possibility and trust that Christ still sends us out to proclaim freedom. The Kingdom of God is near.

-Reverend Betsy Ouellette Zierden, United Methodist

Reflection Questions

1. Betsy describes the apostles "vibrating with possibility, their hearts alive with joy and trembling with fear." When have you felt this same mixture of excitement and trepidation after receiving spiritual authority or insight through expanded consciousness? How do you carry both the joy and the trembling?
2. "At some point faith asks for more than research and reason, it asks for a leap." What leap has your spiritual journey required of you? How do you balance prudent preparation with the radical trust that healing sometimes demands?
3. Betsy shares how she entered the medicine world because her "soul was aching" and discovered "demons of despair loosening their grip." What originally called you to seek healing or expansion? How has that initial wound or longing transformed into a gift you can offer others?

Spiritual Practice for the Week

This week, practice "sending meditation." Each morning, sit quietly and recall a moment when you felt divinely authorized or empowered, perhaps during a mystical experience, in prayer, or through medicine work. Feel that authority alive in your body again.

Then ask: "Where am I being sent today?" Listen for simple acts of healing rather than grand missions. Maybe you're sent to offer presence to a struggling friend, to speak truth in a difficult conversation, or simply to embody joy in a weary world.

Like the woman on the plane trusting God to provide, practice moving through your day with less preparation and more presence. Notice when you want to over-control versus when you can step forward in faith. Each evening, reflect: "How did I give freely what I freely received?"

Journal Prompts

Betsy imagines herself "among the Twelve—fragile yet empowered, naïve perhaps, but also alive with possibility." Write yourself into this scene. What would it feel like to be personally commissioned by Jesus to heal and liberate? What specific authorities or gifts from your own journey would he name and send you out with?

"Not everyone will hear this as good news, but those who are ready will recognize it." Write about a time when you shared your healing or spiritual insight and it wasn't received. How did you learn to discern who is ready to hear? How do you stay faithful to your truth while respecting others' readiness?

PROPER 7 (PENTECOST 5): FEAR NO ONE

The Reading

"A disciple is not above the teacher nor a slave above the master; it is enough for the disciple to be like the teacher and the slave like the master. If they have called the master of the house Beelzebul, how much more will they malign those of his household!

Whom to Fear
"So have no fear of them, for nothing is covered up that will not be uncovered and nothing secret that will not become known. What I say to you in the dark, tell in the light, and what you hear whispered, proclaim from the housetops. Do not fear those who kill the body but cannot kill the soul; rather, fear the one who can destroy both soul and body in hell. Are not two sparrows sold for a penny? Yet not one of them will fall to the ground apart from your Father. And even the hairs of your head are all counted. So do not be afraid; you are of more value than many sparrows.

"Everyone, therefore, who acknowledges me before others, I also will acknowledge before my Father in heaven, but whoever denies me before others, I also will deny before my Father in heaven.

Not Peace, but a Sword
"Do not think that I have come to bring peace to the earth; I have not come to bring peace but a sword.

For I have come to set a man against his father,
and a daughter against her mother,
and a daughter-in-law against her mother-in-law,
and one's foes will be members of one's own household.

Whoever loves father or mother more than me is not worthy of me, and whoever loves son or daughter more than me is not worthy of me, and whoever does not take up the cross and follow me is not worthy of me. Those who find their life will lose it, and those who lose their life for my sake will find it.

-Matthew 10:24–39

Through the Mystical Lens

She cried out to her child, "I don't trust your father. I hate him!" Anger - no, it didn't come. Just immense gratitude. Thank you for releasing me.

Many commentaries attempt to soften the blow of the harsh words spoken by Jesus (attributed to him by the gospel writer?): a radical demand of discipleship—calling followers to prioritize Christ above all, endure suffering, relinquish attachments, and embrace total surrender, even at the cost of familial ties or worldly security.

Transcending and including the theme of following Christ in the unknown, when viewed through the lens of psychedelic experience / plant medicine journey work, his words become a portal into the dissolution of ego—where the self-that-clings, fears, and seeks control is gently surrendered. Holding both love/hate together, dropping both (and ultimately all personal preference), we dance with and set the ego free; a release from old roles, histories, and attachments, allowing the authentic self to awaken beyond separation, fear, and the drive for external approval

Hate points to a mystical freedom: the letting go of egoic bonds and inherited obligations that keep one trapped in old patterns, allowing the total human being to move without hindrance toward complete union and surrender to the Divine.

-Rev. Brent Reynolds, Vine Contemplative Community + Tribe of the Open Heart

Reflection Questions

1. Brent describes responding to angry words with "immense gratitude" for the release they brought. When has someone's harsh truth or difficult confrontation unexpectedly freed you from a burden you didn't know you were carrying?
2. The reflection speaks of "letting go of egoic bonds and inherited obligations that keep one trapped in old patterns." What familial or cultural expectations have you had to release, perhaps with grief, to follow your authentic spiritual path?
3. "Holding both love/hate together, dropping both (and ultimately all personal preference)": when have you experienced this dissolution of preferences in favor of a larger surrendering? What emerged in that spaciousness?

Spiritual Practice for the Week

This week, practice "Releasing the Bonds":

Each morning, identify one relationship or obligation that feels heavy with expectation, history, or unspoken rules. Hold it gently in awareness without trying to fix or flee.

Breathe deeply and imagine this bond as a cord connecting you to the other person or situation. See its color, texture, weight. Notice: Is this cord made of love? Fear? Duty? Old patterns?

Without cutting or violence, imagine the cord becoming lighter, more translucent. It's not severed but transformed: still connected but no longer binding. You can love without clinging, honor without being enslaved.

Throughout the day, when you feel old patterns activating (people-pleasing, rebellion, seeking approval), pause and remember: "I am free to respond from my authentic self, not from inherited roles."

Before sleep, offer gratitude for any moments of freedom you experienced, even if they came through difficult encounters.

Journal Prompts

Brent writes of "mystical freedom" that comes from releasing "inherited obligations that keep one trapped in old patterns." Describe a time when spiritual growth required you to disappoint or even wound those you love. How did you navigate the sword that divides while still holding compassion?

The reflection mentions "the self-that-clings, fears, and seeks control is gently surrendered." Write about an experience, perhaps in ceremony, meditation, or life crisis, when this clinging self dissolved. What did you discover about who you are beyond your roles, fears, and need for control?

PROPER 8 (PENTECOST 6): REWARDS

The Reading

"Whoever welcomes you welcomes me, and whoever welcomes me welcomes the one who sent me. Whoever welcomes a prophet in the name of a prophet will receive a prophet's reward, and whoever welcomes a righteous person in the name of a righteous person will receive the reward of the righteous, and whoever gives even a cup of cold water to one of these little ones in the name of a disciple—truly I tell you, none of these will lose their reward."

-Matthew 10:40-42

Through the Mystical Lens

At the heart of the Christian life is an invitation to receive and to offer radical hospitality: "Whoever welcomes you welcomes me." The Divine Presence is hidden in each arrival—guest, prophet, or cup of cold water—each moment carrying Christ in disguise. Radical hospitality seems to be a core value in Christianity, as well as in the world's other major religions.

The invitation to radical hospitality is all over our sacred texts. We certainly see it in this passage from Matthew's Gospel, we see it in the Emmaus story (Luke 24:13-35) when the invitation to share a meal allows the two men in the story to realize they've been walking with the Risen Christ. In Hebrew Scripture, Genesis 18:1-33 offers one of many examples. In their encounter with the three mysterious guests at the Oaks of Mamre, Sarah and Abraham discovered their sacred calling.

As I was pondering radical hospitality, I couldn't help but remember "The Guest House", a poem from Islam's Sufi tradition written by Rumi in the 13th century. For me, insights like this from other traditions often help deepen my relationship with Jesus.

> *This being human is a guest house. / Every morning a*
> *new arrival./*
> *A joy, a depression, a meanness, / some momentary*
> *awareness comes/*
>   *As an unexpected visitor.*
>
> *Welcome and entertain them all! / Even if they're a crowd*
> *of sorrows,/*
>   *who violently sweep your house / empty of its*
> *furniture, /*
> *still treat each guest honorably. / He may be clearing you*
> *out /*
>   *for some new delight.*
>
> *The dark thought, the shame, the malice, / meet them at*
> *the door laughing, /*
>   *and invite them in.*

Be grateful for whoever comes, / because each has been sent
   as a guide from beyond.

In the context of my own psychedelic experiences, the invitation to radical hospitality takes on deep immediacy. Many hidden guests have visited me—visions, memories, fears, and luminous insights—each demanding acknowledgment rather than resistance. When I have met these experiences with the generous welcome Christ (and Rumi) commend, my inner house becomes a place of communion and ever-increasing integration.

-Hunt Priest, M.Div. Former Episcopal priest.

Reflection Questions

1. Hunt describes "hidden guests" arriving during psychedelic experiences as "visions, memories, fears, and luminous insights, each demanding acknowledgment rather than resistance." Which uninvited guests have appeared in your consciousness during sacred medicine work? How did your response to them shape the journey?

2. The Gospel promises reward for offering "even a cup of cold water to one of these little ones." During integration, how do you extend this same small kindness to the vulnerable parts of yourself that emerge? What happens when you treat your wounded inner children as sacred guests?

3. The reflection suggests that radical hospitality transforms the "inner house" into "a place of communion and ever-increasing integration." Where in your spiritual life do you still bar the door against certain experiences or emotions? What might open if you welcomed everything as a guide from beyond?

Spiritual Practice for the Week

This week, practice "The Guest House Morning Welcome."

Upon waking, before getting out of bed, place your hands on your heart and take three deep breaths. Then mentally open the door of your consciousness and see what has arrived overnight: perhaps anxiety about the day ahead, fragments of dreams, body sensations, or memories stirred by recent inner work.

To each arrival, offer Rumi's greeting: "Welcome and entertain them all." If resistance arises toward any guest, breathe compassion toward both the unwelcome visitor and your desire to close the door. Remember that in God's economy of hospitality, the difficult guest often bears the greatest gift.

Before bed each night, thank all the day's visitors, wanted and unwanted, for their teachings. Notice which guests you're learning to welcome more easily and which still trigger your urge to bolt the door.

Journal Prompts

Hunt shares how "the two men in the story realize they've been walking with the Risen Christ" only after offering hospitality in the Emmaus story. Write about a time when you recognized the sacred nature of an experience only after you had welcomed it fully. What was the stranger that turned out to be Christ in disguise? How long did it take for recognition to dawn?

Rumi writes of sorrows that "violently sweep your house empty of its furniture" yet instructs us to "treat each guest honorably" because "He may be clearing you out for some new delight." Describe a time when a challenging medicine experience or spiritual crisis emptied you of familiar structures. What furniture was swept away? What new delight eventually filled the cleared space? How does this inform your current relationship with difficult passages?

PROPER 9 (PENTECOST 7): COME TO ME AND REST

The Reading

"But to what will I compare this generation? It is like children sitting in the marketplaces and calling to one another,

'We played the flute for you, and you did not dance;
we wailed, and you did not mourn.'

"For John came neither eating nor drinking, and they say, 'He has a demon'; the Son of Man came eating and drinking, and they say, 'Look, a glutton and a drunkard, a friend of tax collectors and sinners!' Yet wisdom is vindicated by her deeds."

Jesus Thanks His Father

At that time Jesus said, "I thank you, Father, Lord of heaven and earth, because you have hidden these things from the wise and the intelligent and have revealed them to infants; yes, Father, for such was your gracious will. All things have been handed over to me by my Father, and no one knows the Son except the Father, and no one knows the Father except the Son and anyone to whom the Son chooses to reveal him.

"Come to me, all you who are weary and are carrying heavy burdens, and I will give you rest. Take my yoke upon you, and learn from me, for I am gentle and humble in heart, and you will find rest for your souls. For my yoke is easy, and my burden is light."

Matthew 11:16-19, 25-30

Through the Mystical Lens

Part of the drive to leave this material, grinding, soul-crushing world is our weariness. The struggle to rise above begins to extend to the depths of our spirit and we seek to go further. We seek out spiritual 'growth', personal 'evolution', to go beyond the veil of illusion and see the true reality. Mystics, spiritual gurus, and trippers strive to make sense of a world that doesn't make much sense at all. Material survival, the spiritual quest, the perfection of the personality - it is all so much work. For what? Why?

The mystical moment, such as it is, may simply be the feeling of giving up all the work, all the striving, all the attempts to become more, greater than, higher in a spiritual and personal sense. The implication in this passage is that Jesus has done all the work needed for all of that. You? You just need to rest, to take on the yoke of the easy and the light.

I believe part of what kills the mystical sensibility, part of what destroys our creative and imaginative faith, is taking what we think we believe so seriously. What if you took what you believe lightly and held it like an easy yoke that provided rest and comfort, rather than work and extension and exhaustion?

-Rev. Dr. Seth Jones, Congregational Church

Reflection Questions

1. Jesus says "wisdom is vindicated by her deeds." What fruits have emerged in your life from releasing spiritual striving and accepting rest?
2. Seth asks if your church community is "easy and restful." When have you experienced faith community as burden versus balm? What made the difference?
3. Jesus was criticized as "a glutton and a drunkard, a friend of tax collectors and sinners" for living with joy. How has the fear of judgment kept you from embracing a lighter, more playful faith?

Spiritual Practice for the Week

Practice "Laying Down the Heavy Yoke":

Each morning this week, identify one spiritual "should" that exhausts you: perhaps maintaining perfect prayer habits, understanding all doctrine, or earning your way to heaven. Hold this burden in your hands, feeling its weight.

Then literally set it down. Place your hands on the ground or a table, releasing this burden physically. Say aloud: "Jesus says his yoke is easy and his burden is light."

Throughout the day, when you catch yourself picking up spiritual striving, pause. Take three breaths and ask: "Is this the easy yoke or the heavy one?"

Each evening, practice one playful spiritual act: dance to sacred music, draw a prayer instead of speaking it, or simply laugh at the divine comedy of existence. Notice how rest feels in your body.

Journal Prompts

Seth notes that "taking what we believe so seriously" can kill our mystical sensibility. Write about a spiritual belief or practice you've held with white-knuckled intensity. What would it mean to hold this same truth lightly, like a bird rather than a stone?

The reflection asks: "Why do you want to be taken seriously?" Explore what you fear would happen if people saw you as spiritually playful, even foolish. What freedom might await on the other side of that fear?

PROPER 10 (PENTECOST 8): THE PARABLE OF THE SOWER

The Reading

The Parable of the Sower

That same day Jesus went out of the house and sat beside the sea. Such great crowds gathered around him that he got into a boat and sat there, while the whole crowd stood on the beach. And he told them many things in parables, saying: "Listen! A sower went out to sow. And as he sowed, some seeds fell on a path, and the birds came and ate them up. Other seeds fell on rocky ground, where they did not have much soil, and they sprang up quickly, since they had no depth of soil. But when the sun rose, they were scorched, and since they had no root, they withered away. Other seeds fell among thorns, and the thorns grew up and choked them. Other seeds fell on good soil and brought forth grain, some a hundredfold, some sixty, some thirty. If you have ears, hear!"

The Parable of the Sower Explained

"Hear, then, the parable of the sower. When anyone hears the word of the kingdom and does not understand it, the evil one comes and snatches away what is sown in the heart; this is what was sown on the path. As for what was sown on rocky ground, this is the one who hears the word and immediately receives it with joy, yet such a person has no root but endures only for a while, and when trouble or persecution arises on account of the word, that person immediately falls away. As for what was sown among thorns, this is the one who hears the word, but the cares of this age and the lure of wealth choke the word, and it yields nothing. But as for what was sown on good soil, this is the one who hears the word and understands it, who indeed bears fruit and yields in one case a hundredfold, in another sixty, and in another thirty."

-Matthew 13:1–9, 18–23

Through the Mystical Lens

Jesus is sitting in a boat because the crowd is pressing in. People are hungry for something real, and He gives them… a story about dirt.

Only Jesus would do that.

A sower goes out and just starts throwing seed like he has more than he knows what to do with. It lands everywhere — on the road, in gravel, tangled up in thorns, and in the kind of soil that farmers brag about over dinner. No strategy. No spreadsheets. No trying to "get it right." Just wild, generous scattering.

For years I heard this parable like a spiritual report card. Which soil am I today? Passing or failing? But lately, I've begun to wonder if the point isn't the soil at all… but the Sower.

Because this Sower doesn't seem bothered by where the seed lands. He just throws with both hands — like the possibility of life is too urgent to waste time filtering out the "unsuitable" places.

Meister Eckhart once wrote, *"The seed of God is in us: Pear seeds grow into pear trees; Hazel seeds into hazel trees; And God seeds into God."*

There's something already planted inside — divine potential, God-DNA — even in the places we've written off as unproductive or broken or too busy or too late.

And yes… soil matters. We know this. Some of our inner landscape has been trampled by life — hard-packed by expectations, disappointments, loss.

Some places are thin — a burst of newness that can't quite hold through the heat.

Some places feel thorny — where worry chokes joy before it has a chance to bloom.

And then there are pockets of good soil we didn't even know were there until something green started pushing through.

In the ancient world, seed often hit the ground *before* the plow turned the earth. The work came after. The soil wasn't judged first — it was trusted, tended, held.

The spiritual life is like that. Sometimes grace arrives suddenly — like a rush of insight or a widened consciousness — and other times it works slowly, turning over what has hardened, pulling back what chokes, helping roots sink deep.

The miracle is that the Sower never stops scattering. Never gives up on the field. Never withholds. Somehow, in the hidden places, God-seed becomes God-life… thirty, sixty, a hundredfold.

-Rev. Dr. Andrea F. Smith, United Methodist

Reflection Questions

1. Andrea suggests the ancient practice where "seed often hit the ground before the plow turned the earth." When has grace arrived in your life before you felt ready or worthy to receive it? How did the "plowing" come after?
2. The reflection describes the Sower as unbothered by where seed lands, just throwing "with both hands." When have you experienced this kind of unconditional divine generosity, especially in your "unsuitable" places?
3. "God seeds into God," writes Meister Eckhart. What divine potential have you discovered growing in the parts of yourself you'd written off as unproductive, broken, or too busy?

Spiritual Practice for the Week

This week, practice "Receiving the Seed":

Each morning, open your hands in a gesture of receiving. Take three deep breaths and imagine divine seeds falling into your palms, not just into your "good soil" but everywhere, even the places you've judged as too hard, too shallow, or too thorny.

Throughout the day, notice when you catch yourself evaluating your spiritual "productivity." When self-judgment arises ("I'm too distracted," "I'm not growing fast enough," "I keep failing"), pause and remember: The Sower is still scattering seeds right here, right now, in this exact condition.

Each evening, place your hand on different parts of your body (head, heart, belly) and bless each area: "Seeds are planted here. Something is growing, even if I can't see it yet."

At week's end, journal about what shifted when you stopped evaluating your soil and started trusting the Sower's generosity.

Journal Prompts

Andrea writes of "pockets of good soil we didn't even know were there until something green started pushing through." Describe a time when growth emerged from an unexpected place in your life, perhaps during difficulty, dryness, or distraction. What conditions allowed this hidden fertility to reveal itself?

The reflection mentions how "worry chokes joy before it has a chance to bloom." Identify one area where thorns of anxiety or busyness are choking potential growth. Without trying to fix it, simply acknowledge what's happening there. What would it mean to trust that the Sower keeps scattering seeds even in your thorniest ground?

PROPER 11 (PENTECOST 9): THE PARABLE OF THE WEEDS AMONG THE WHEAT

The Reading

The Parable of Weeds among the Wheat

He put before them another parable: "The kingdom of heaven may be compared to someone who sowed good seed in his field, but while everybody was asleep an enemy came and sowed weeds among the wheat and then went away. So when the plants came up and bore grain, then the weeds appeared as well. And the slaves of the householder came and said to him, 'Master, did you not sow good seed in your field? Where, then, did these weeds come from?' He answered, 'An enemy has done this.' The slaves said to him, 'Then do you want us to go and gather them?' But he replied, 'No, for in gathering the weeds you would uproot the wheat along with them. Let both of them grow together until the harvest, and at harvest time I will tell the reapers, Collect the weeds first and bind them in bundles to be burned, but gather the wheat into my barn.' "

Jesus Explains the Parable of the Weeds
Then he left the crowds and went into the house. And his disciples approached him, saying, "Explain to us the parable of the weeds of the field." He answered, "The one who sows the good seed is the Son of Man; the field is the world, and the good seed are the children of the kingdom; the weeds are the children of the evil one, and the enemy who sowed them is the devil; the harvest is the end of the age, and the reapers are angels. Just as the weeds are collected and burned up with fire, so will it be at the end of the age. The Son of Man will send his angels, and they will collect out of his kingdom all causes of sin and all evildoers, and they will throw them into the furnace of fire, where there will be weeping and gnashing of teeth. Then the righteous will shine like the sun in the kingdom of their Father. Let anyone with ears listen!

-Matthew 13:24–30, 36–43

Through the Mystical Lens

"Someone sowed some really good seed in a field," Jesus said. "And in the middle of the night, an enemy sneaked in and tossed weeds willy-nilly all around the field."

"Wait a minute, Jesus," the disciples said. Or someone in the crowd said. Or I said. Or you said. "You're saying that someone was so mad at someone else that they infested their crop in the middle of the night? That's wacky."

"Yep," Jesus said, "That's wacky. Much of life is wacky."

"Who would do that," I asked. Or you asked. Or a disciple. Or a member of the crowd asked.

"An enemy," Jesus said.

"Hang on, Jesus! Eight chapters earlier, didn't you just say,' Love your enemies'?

"Yes, I did."

"That's pretty funny. I mean, what if we're not supposed to have enemies?"

"Yeah, it's all pretty funny," Jesus said.

"Okay, tell me more."

"Well, when the crops bloomed there were weeds everywhere. And when the slaves came to the owner…"

"Slow down, slow down. Slaves? I still can't wrap my head around the idea that people once thought it was okay to own slaves."

"I know, right," said Jesus. "It's all a big ole jumble."

"Yeah it is. Life is a big ole jumble."

"You're catching on," said Jesus.

"I don't know. Maybe. I'm trying to pay attention. Trying to keep up."

"Let anyone with ears listen."

"Wait, who are you talking to, Jesus? The disciples? The crowd? Me? The people who are reading this book?"

"Yes," Jesus said, winking. "Yes."

-Rev. Dr. Timothy Tutt, United Church of Christ

Reflection Questions

1. When have you experienced the divine winking at you through life's absurdity, those moments when the "big ole jumble" suddenly reveals itself as sacred play? How does

recognizing this cosmic humor deepen rather than diminish your faith?

2. "Let anyone with ears listen," Jesus says, speaking to disciples, crowds, and readers across time. After your consciousness has expanded, how do you hear scripture's multiple layers simultaneously? What meanings only become audible after you've touched the infinite?

3. The parable presents enemies, judgment, and final sorting: elements that may feel foreign after experiencing universal love. How do you hold these tensions without dismissing either the text or your own direct knowing?

Spiritual Practice for the Week

This week, practice "wheat and weed meditation" with a playful twist.

Sit quietly and bring to mind a quality you judge as "wheat" (good) in yourself. Hold it without grasping. Then bring to mind a "weed" quality. Hold it without rejection.

As you sit with both, imagine having a conversation with them like the dialogue in this week's reflection. Ask your inner wheat: "Wait a minute, are you really all good?" Ask your inner weed: "Hang on, who says you're all bad?" Listen for their responses. You might discover your wheat has shadows and your weeds bear unexpected gifts.

Notice how they've grown together, roots intertwined in the "big ole jumble" of your being. Practice holding both with equanimity and even humor. Can you sense the divine winking at you through your own contradictions?

End by resting in the ground of being that nourishes both. Throughout your day, when you notice yourself wanting to uproot something in others or yourself, pause. Ask: "Is this the harvest time, or am I being called to patient tending?" Remember: even Jesus insists the sorting isn't our job.

Journal Prompts

In the imagined conversation, someone (maybe you) keeps interrupting Jesus: "Wait a minute!" and "Hang on!" Write about a time when you wanted to interrupt a spiritual teaching or scripture because it didn't match your expanded understanding. What happened when you let yourself question out loud?

"Yeah, it's all pretty funny," Jesus says in the dialogue, acknowledging life's absurdity. Describe a moment when you glimpsed the divine comedy, when the "big ole jumble" of existence revealed itself as somehow both messy and perfect. How does finding God's playfulness in the chaos change how you read difficult parables like this one?

PROPER 12 (PENTECOST 10): THE PARABLES OF THE MUSTARD SEED AND THE YEAST

The Reading

The Parable of the Mustard Seed
He put before them another parable: "The kingdom of heaven is like a mustard seed that someone took and sowed in his field; it is the smallest of all the seeds, but when it has grown it is the greatest of shrubs and becomes a tree, so that the birds of the air come and make nests in its branches."

The Parable of the Yeast
He told them another parable: "The kingdom of heaven is like yeast that a woman took and mixed in with three measures of flour until all of it was leavened."

Three Parables
"The kingdom of heaven is like treasure hidden in a field, which a man found and reburied; then in his joy he goes and sells all that he has and buys that field.

   "Again, the kingdom of heaven is like a merchant in search

of fine pearls; on finding one pearl of great value, he went and sold all that he had and bought it.

"Again, the kingdom of heaven is like a net that was thrown into the sea and caught fish of every kind; when it was full, they drew it ashore, sat down, and put the good into baskets but threw out the bad. So it will be at the end of the age. The angels will come out and separate the evil from the righteous and throw them into the furnace of fire, where there will be weeping and gnashing of teeth.

Treasures New and Old
"Have you understood all this?" They answered, "Yes." And he said to them, "Therefore every scribe who has become a disciple in the kingdom of heaven is like the master of a household who brings out of his treasure what is new and what is old." When Jesus had finished these parables, he left that place.

-Matthew 13:31–33, 44–52

Through the Mystical Lens

Whenever we see Jesus describe the Kingdom of God in this passage, he chooses something small — a seed, a pinch of yeast, a single pearl hidden in the sand. He defies the expectations of the dramatic and the grand. He emphasizes that the Kingdom comes hidden from our perception, working in silence until it remakes everything anew.

This is how awakening actually happens. The Kingdom is not something that happens in a huge event: say, a political takeover or a sweeping election, but it is something already germinating within us — an idea and intention seeded so deep it may first look like nothing at all. A mustard seed is not impressive, but it contains a future tree. Yeast disappears into the dough, but leavening the whole loaf. Even in experiences with sacred medicines, one idea is that the *medicine is already within you*. What we encounter and what is healing was inside us all along. In a sense, we don't need to be "saved" in order to see and be a part of the Kingdom. We only need to see, to hear, to understand, to connect.

And like the merchant joyfully selling all he has, the soul knows when it has stumbled upon something worthwhile. Our encounters with the Kingdom have a way of redefining value. When you taste what is real, you gladly release what once felt essential.

Even the sorting of the fish, where the "good" are kept, the "bad" thrown out can be read not as judging people, but rather discarding destructive patterns, beliefs, and ways of thinking. The Kingdom of God does not destroy persons, it transforms them. The Kingdom happens when the false ego loosens its hold, and the soul discards what cannot breathe in the light. This is the end of the age happening *within you*: an inner apocalypse that creates and transforms, becoming the Kingdom in the flesh.

The Kingdom is not far away. It is already fermenting in the hidden places inside yourself. The Kingdom is waiting and growing within you. Nurture and discover its fruits.

-Rev. B. Jeffrey Vidt, United Church of Christ

Reflection Questions

1. Jeffrey asks about experiencing "something small" that revealed itself as sacred. When has a tiny seed of experience: a fleeting moment, a whisper of intuition, grown into a life-changing understanding?
2. The reflection mentions "yeast" quietly working within. What transformation is fermenting in your depths right now, perhaps so subtle you barely notice its sacred work?
3. When have you experienced an "inner apocalypse": old patterns being sorted and discarded while your authentic self

emerged? What made you willing to release what no longer served?

Spiritual Practice for the Week

This week, practice "Sacred Noticing of the Small":

Each day, choose one tiny, overlooked element of your world: a leaf's vein pattern, background traffic sounds, steam rising from your tea, the sensation of fingertips touching any surface. Something so ordinary it usually escapes attention.

Hold your full awareness on this small thing for one complete minute. As you observe, repeat silently: "The Kingdom is growing here."

Resist the urge to make it meaningful. Your role is simply to remain present long enough to witness its becoming. Trust that the Kingdom ferments beneath ordinary surfaces.

Notice if this practice of honoring the small shifts how you move through your day. Does the world reveal more of its hidden sacred nature?

At week's end, reflect: What did sustained attention to the tiny teach you about how God moves?

Journal Prompts

Jeffrey suggests that "what we encounter and what is healing was inside us all along." Write about a time when an experience (perhaps with medicine, prayer, or crisis) revealed capacities for healing you didn't know you carried. How did discovering this inner treasure change your understanding of salvation?

The reflection reframes the "sorting of fish" as discarding destructive patterns rather than judging people. What beliefs, behaviors, or ways of thinking have you "thrown out" as incompatible with your emerging authentic self? How did this inner sorting feel like death and resurrection happening simultaneously?

PROPER 13 (PENTECOST 11): FEEDING THE FIVE THOUSAND

The Reading

Now when Jesus heard this, he withdrew from there in a boat to a deserted place by himself. But when the crowds heard it, they followed him on foot from the towns. When he went ashore, he saw a great crowd, and he had compassion for them and cured their sick. When it was evening, the disciples came to him and said, "This is a deserted place, and the hour is now late; send the crowds away so that they may go into the villages and buy food for themselves." Jesus said to them, "They need not go away; you give them something to eat." They replied, "We have nothing here but five loaves and two fish." And he said, "Bring them here to me." Then he ordered the crowds to sit down on the grass. Taking the five loaves and the two fish, he looked up to heaven and blessed and broke the loaves and gave them to the disciples, and the disciples gave them to the crowds. And all ate and were filled, and they took up what was left over of the broken pieces, twelve baskets full.

And those who ate were about five thousand men, besides women and children.

-Matthew 14:13–21

Through the Mystical Lens

Jesus learns of the horrific murder of his cousin John the Baptist by the cruelty of King Herod and in his state of shock and grief, he engages in the self-care of the solitude of roadtrip (boat ride) to a remote place. Alas, throngs of people meet him there. They too were in various states of despair, brokenness, grief, and oppression. They too were travelling to a remote place to seek solace as self-care. The context is one of dis-ease and perceived barren emptiness. Jesus has compassion for them and heals much sickness. A focus on one individual and seeking what benefit might be there results in increased wholeness and well-being.

The disciples rightly notice another real need, the hunger of that mass of humanity. Jesus tells them to handle it themselves. He shifts the focus from the individual him, to the individuality of each of them. They respond protesting that they "have nothing" - other than a few individual items of food. Jesus has them focus on those individual things, invites God's blessing on each of them, and has them feed the masses.

It is discovered that there was more than enough food for everyone to be fed - including the 5,000 individual men, as well as the no doubt additional at least 10,000 other individuals who the Gospel writer makes a point to include - the individual women and individual children.

Perhaps the miracle was getting masses of people to shift from a scarcity mindset that only sees lack, to one where appreciation of individual small bits of food that were in the possession of that throng mattered - mattered to the point where they could share them with each other and meet their collective needs.

Part of this miracle is realizing that we already have all that we need in life. That we can turn to ourselves, and each other, and notice and appreciate whatever small thing that we may have and trust that it matters and that it's worthy of sharing.

Psychedelic journeys are often like that. They may include colorful images, visions, and patterns, and we might prefer it when they happen. Yet journeys that don't involve those are often just as profound and transformative. I think of times when there are colorful patterns that catch my eye, but if I instead look toward the seemingly empty and barren portion of my field of sight, there often is at least one small dot of light or color, one small fractal of a fractal, of a fractal. And, when I chose to focus on it, and give it my attention, it almost always leads to a profound insight or blessing that I was needing. Sometimes they become portals to vast richness. Such journeys are analogies like the parables Jesus told, or the stories about him.

Mahatma Gandhi said, *"Whatever you do in life will seem insignificant but it is very important that you do it because you can't know. You can't ever really know the meaning of your life. And you don't need to. Every life has a meaning, whether it lasts one hundred years or one hundred seconds. Every life, and every death, changes the world in its own way. You can't know. So don't take it for granted."* Jesus says that too. What say you?

-*Rev. Roger Wolsey, United Methodist Church, Spiritual Director*

Reflection Questions

1. Roger notes Jesus needed self-care after learning of John the Baptist's murder. When has your own grief or shock required solitude, only to find others drawn to your wounded

presence? How did serving from brokenness change both you and those you served?

2. The reflection suggests the miracle was shifting from scarcity mindset to recognizing "we already have all that we need." What small, overlooked resources in your life await blessing and sharing? When has abundance emerged from apparent lack?

3. Roger describes focusing on "one small dot of light" in seemingly empty space during journeys. When have you found profound insight by attending to what seemed insignificant or barren rather than the colorful and obvious?

Spiritual Practice for the Week

This week, practice "Finding Fullness in the Fragment":

Each day, identify something you consider insufficient: perhaps limited time, energy, money, or ability. Hold this "five loaves and two fish" awareness without judgment.

Sit quietly with this perceived lack. Instead of focusing on what's missing, turn full attention to what IS present, however small. Like Roger's "fractal of a fractal," zoom in on the tiniest portion of what you have.

Bless this fragment. Say aloud: "This is enough to begin. This matters." Then take one small action with what you have, trusting it to multiply through sharing.

Each evening, notice: How did attending to the small shift your experience? Where did unexpected abundance appear? What hungry crowd (inner or outer) was fed by your willingness to offer your fragments?

Journal Prompts

Roger writes about Jesus telling the disciples "you give them something to eat" and their protest that they "have nothing." Describe a time when you were asked to give from your emptiness. What did you discover you actually possessed when forced to look closely? How did the act of giving transform both the gift and the giver?

The reflection connects psychedelic journeys to Gospel parables, noting how focusing on "seemingly empty and barren" portions often yields profound insight. Write about an experience (in journey or life) when the void, the absence, or the darkness became your teacher. What blessing emerged from staying present with emptiness rather than chasing fullness?

PROPER 14 (PENTECOST 12): JESUS WALKS ON THE WATER

The Reading

Immediately he made the disciples get into a boat and go on ahead to the other side, while he dismissed the crowds. And after he had dismissed the crowds, he went up the mountain by himself to pray. When evening came, he was there alone, but by this time the boat, battered by the waves, was far from the land, for the wind was against them. And early in the morning he came walking toward them on the sea. But when the disciples saw him walking on the sea, they were terrified, saying, "It is a ghost!" And they cried out in fear. But immediately Jesus spoke to them and said, "Take heart, it is I; do not be afraid."

Peter answered him, "Lord, if it is you, command me to come to you on the water." He said, "Come." So Peter got out of the boat, started walking on the water, and came toward Jesus. But when he noticed the strong wind, he became frightened, and, beginning to sink, he cried out, "Lord, save me!" Jesus immediately reached out his hand and caught him, saying to him, "You of little faith, why did you doubt?" When they got into the boat, the wind ceased. And those in the boat worshiped him, saying, "Truly you are the Son of God."

-Matthew 14:22–33

Through the Mystical Lens

Water is a gift that sustains life, and for many spiritual and religious communities, water is the primordial source from which life was created. For contemporary Christian mystic Cynthia Borgeault water is symbolic of unitive and undifferentiated consciousness and the miracle of walking on water is about dwelling within this unitive state. The waves of the water are symbolic of the tumultuous churning, reactive egoic self, while the still depths represent the calm, witnessing presence which remains unshaken by the emotional and psychic storms of the personal self. The disciples begin to panic at the stormy waters, and Peter sinks beneath the surface because he descends into fear and doubt, losing his vital connection to the unitive Christ-consciousness.

For Christians this unitive, sustaining, and nondual quality of water that sustains us above the storms of life is divine love. The water ritual of baptism affirms that we belong to love and are sustained in love, through Christ. Through entheogenic practices, or in deep meditation, we may find ourselves lost in the rough waters of the mind and emotions. But knowing that we can return to this unitive, eternal, source of life can provide stability, confidence and support to navigate the storms. We can remember that we were born in divine love and the hand of Christ that reached out to Peter in his struggle is also available to us when we become lost or disconnected.

-Jamie Beachy, MDiv, PhD, Mennonite

Reflection Questions

Jamie asks how Jesus's response to stormy seas enables him to help others. When have you found that your own grounding in contemplative practice allowed you to be a steady presence for someone in crisis?

The reflection describes water as "unitive and undifferentiated consciousness." When have you experienced yourself as both the waves (reactive ego) and the depths (witnessing presence) simultaneously? How did holding both change your relationship to emotional storms?

Peter sinks when he "descends into fear and doubt, losing his vital connection to the unitive Christ-consciousness." What pulls you out of unitive awareness? What helps you remember the hand reaching toward you?

Spiritual Practice for the Week

This week, practice "Waves and Depths":

Find a comfortable position and settle into meditation. As thoughts and emotions arise, visualize them as waves on an ocean's surface: some gentle, some stormy.

Rather than trying to calm the waves, drop your awareness beneath them. Feel for the still depths that remain constant regardless of surface conditions. Rest there for 10-15 minutes daily.

When you notice yourself being pulled up into the waves (reactive thoughts, strong emotions), gently return to the depths. No judgment, just a soft return to the deep.

Throughout your day, when storms arise (conflict, anxiety, overwhelm), pause and ask: "Can I touch the depths even while the waves crash?" Practice maintaining contact with both dimensions of experience.

Notice how this dual awareness affects your ability to extend love to others in their storms.

Journal Prompts

Jamie writes about "the hand of Christ that reached out to Peter" being available to us. Describe a time when you were sinking in fear or doubt and felt something, whether you call it Christ, Love, or Presence, reach for you. How did you recognize this reaching? What allowed you to grasp it?

The reflection connects baptismal waters with "belonging to love." Write about your relationship to water as a spiritual element. How has water appeared in your mystical experiences: as threat, cleansing, dissolution, or unity? What has water taught you about the nature of consciousness?

PROPER 15 (PENTECOST 13): THE CANAANITE WOMAN'S FAITH

The Reading

Jesus left that place and went away to the district of Tyre and Sidon. Just then a Canaanite woman from that region came out and started shouting, "Have mercy on me, Lord, Son of David; my daughter is tormented by a demon." But he did not answer her at all. And his disciples came and urged him, saying, "Send her away, for she keeps shouting after us." He answered, "I was sent only to the lost sheep of the house of Israel." But she came and knelt before him, saying, "Lord, help me." He answered, "It is not fair to take the children's food and throw it to the dogs." She said, "Yes, Lord, yet even the dogs eat the crumbs that fall from their masters' table." Then Jesus answered her, "Woman, great is your faith! Let it be done for you as you wish." And her daughter was healed from that moment.

-Matthew 15:21–28

Through the Mystical Lens

Can the divine mind be changed? This story seems to imply that it can. Jesus, the one also called *Emmanuel* - God with us, heard the Canaanite woman's plea in such a way as to expand both his calling and his consciousness. Was Jesus sent to save "the lost sheep of Israel?" Of course he was. Matthew's gospel begins with a lengthy genealogy connecting the dots to Jesus as the rightful heir to the title Messiah. From Abraham to David, from David to Babylon, and from Babylon to Joseph, the Hebrew story is his story. It's in his heritage.

But whenever Jesus's efforts to find his own voice gets too complicated, he heads for the countryside. This is where he meets a woman filled with desperation for her daughter's well being.

The Canaanite woman doesn't just make a request. She shouts at Jesus! And when he ignores her, she shouts some more. She calls out for mercy from the "Son of David." I wonder if the taste in her mouth was sweet out of respect for Jesus or bitter out of scorn for her people. Harkening back to King David is a reminder that David was the yearned for, God-blessed monarch who ruled over a united Israelite Kingdom. But as with all tribal or nationalistic land acquisitions, in the end there were the conquerors (Israelites) and the conquered (Canaanites).

That history cannot be ignored if we are to understand what is happening here. The revered "Son of David" gets schooled by this insignificant Canaanite woman. No one would have batted an eye if Jesus walked away. No one questioned his comment, "It's not fair to take the children's food and throw it to the dogs." That's what he was supposed to say.

With her voice, she persisted, and by reorienting Jesus' insult, she resisted. *Even the dogs get the crumbs that fall under the master's table, Jesus.* This woke Jesus up. His calling wasn't expansive enough. His consciousness made room for a bigger understanding, a more compassionate worldview. Following the awakening she inspired in him, he accepted her plea and healed her daughter.

Can we really change the god-given truth? When it has belittled others, most certainly we can.

-Rev. Kerra Becker English, Presbyterian

Reflection Questions

1. Kerra asks: "When have you woken up because of someone else's disarming comment to you?" Reflect on a time when someone from the margins of your awareness expanded your consciousness and compassion through their persistence.
2. The reflection suggests Jesus's consciousness "made room for a bigger understanding, a more compassionate worldview." When has your spiritual journey required you to expand beyond inherited boundaries of who deserves healing or inclusion?
3. "Why do women have to beg, plead, and shout to have their pain heard?" Consider how expanded consciousness work, whether through prayer, medicine, or activism, might help dissolve the barriers that force some to shout while others are heard in whispers.

Spiritual Practice for the Week

This week, practice "Sacred Interruption":

Each day, notice who or what you instinctively dismiss, ignore, or categorize as "not my concern": the person asking for money, the difficult relative, the political "other," the part of yourself you reject.

When you catch yourself in dismissal, pause. Take three breaths and ask: "What if this interruption is sacred? What if this person/situation is here to expand my consciousness?"

Don't force yourself to engage if it's unsafe or unwise. But stay present to the discomfort of having your boundaries questioned. Notice: What assumptions are being challenged? What inherited prejudices are showing themselves?

Each evening, journal briefly: "Today, I was interrupted by ___ and I noticed my consciousness expanding/contracting in this way: ___"

By week's end, reflect on how these interruptions might be invitations to a more expansive faith.

Journal Prompts

The Canaanite woman "reoriented Jesus' insult" about dogs into an argument for inclusion. Write about a time when you transformed an experience of rejection or insult into an opportunity for expanded awareness, yours or others'. What gave you the courage to persist?

Kerra writes of Jesus being "schooled by this insignificant Canaanite woman." Explore a moment when someone society deemed "insignificant" taught you something profound about God, justice, or love. How did their wisdom change your understanding of whose voices carry divine truth?

PROPER 16 (PENTECOST 14): PETER'S DECLARATION ABOUT JESUS

The Reading

Now when Jesus came into the district of Caesarea Philippi, he asked his disciples, "Who do people say that the Son of Man is?" And they said, "Some say John the Baptist but others Elijah and still others Jeremiah or one of the prophets." He said to them, "But who do you say that I am?" Simon Peter answered, "You are the Messiah, the Son of the living God." And Jesus answered him, "Blessed are you, Simon son of Jonah! For flesh and blood has not revealed this to you but my Father in heaven. And I tell you, you are Peter, and on this rock I will build my church, and the gates of Hades will not prevail against it. I will give you the keys of the kingdom of heaven, and whatever you bind on earth will be bound in heaven, and whatever you loose on earth will be loosed in heaven." Then he sternly ordered the disciples not to tell anyone that he was the Messiah.

-Matthew 16:13–20

Through the Mystical Lens

"Who do *you* say I am?"

Hilary of Poitiers understood: "It was a secret he was asking about, into which the faith of those who believe ought to extend itself." Not dogmatic certainty or correctness. A *secret*—something hidden, a mystery waiting to be unveiled through direct encounter.

"Flesh and blood didn't reveal that to you." Peter's recognition didn't come through human transmission—not study, not human logic or authority, not secondhand reports. The Father pulled back the veil. This is *theoria*, direct seeing. *Gnosis* in its truest sense.

Those who've touched mystical depths know this distinction. You can read every book about the Ocean and become an expert oceanographer. Then one day—in contemplative prayer, in sacred medicine, in overwhelming grace—you're not reading or even reasoning anymore. You're drowning. The Living God isn't a concept to grasp and define but Presence that shatters all grasping.

And then Jesus speaks the promise: "The gates of Hades will not prevail."

The early church knew this terrain intimately. Between Good Friday and Pascha, Christ descends into Hades (hell) itself—not to be trapped but to shatter the gates from within. Every mystical journey mirrors this pattern. Ego death. Dark night. The terrifying dissolution where everything you thought was solid melts away.

The gates of hell can't hold. Not because we avoid darkness but because Christ has already descended there, already broken through. When medicine takes you down into your own underworld, when prayer strips away every defense, when you face the void—*He is already there.* The light shines in the darkness, and the darkness cannot overcome it.

"On this rock I will build my church." Not on rationalistic propositions or intellectual certainty. On the faith born from direct encounter with the Living One—the faith that survives the descent, that knows death isn't final, that the gates of hell cannot hold.

Who do *you* say He is?

-The Very Reverend Dr Geoffrey Ready, Orthodox Church

Reflection Questions

1. Fr Geoffrey distinguishes between theological expertise and "drowning" in the Living God. When have you moved from knowing about the divine to being overwhelmed by direct Presence? What had to be surrendered for this shift?
2. The reflection states that Christ "descends into Hades itself—not to be trapped but to shatter the gates from within." When have you experienced your own descent into darkness becoming a liberation rather than imprisonment?
3. "Flesh and blood didn't reveal that to you." Peter's recognition came through direct unveiling. What spiritual truths have come to you not through study or reasoning but through sudden knowing? How do you trust such revelation?

Spiritual Practice for the Week

This week, practice "The Descent and Recognition":

Each morning, sit in silence and ask: "Who do you say I am?" Turn the question inward: let the Divine ask this of you. Who does God say you are, beyond all your self-definitions?

When you encounter darkness this week (fear, doubt, grief, confusion), remember: "The gates of hell cannot hold." Instead of fleeing the descent, breathe into it. Christ has already gone there. You're not alone in your underworld.

Before sleep, rest your hand on your heart and feel for the "rock" within: the place where you've been met by Living Presence rather than your certainties or achievements. This is the foundation that survives every shattering.

Once this week, if possible, immerse yourself in water: shower, bath, ocean, rain. As the water surrounds you, let yourself move from thinking about God to "drowning" in Presence, even for a moment.

Journal Prompts

Fr Geoffrey writes of "the terrifying dissolution where everything you thought was solid melts away." Describe such a dissolution in your own journey, whether through loss, medicine work, or spiritual crisis. What remained when everything else melted? What was revealed in that emptiness?

The reflection speaks of faith "that survives the descent, that knows death isn't final." Write about a time when you discovered something indestructible within yourself precisely through an experience of dying: ego death, loss of identity, dark night. How did this change your understanding of resurrection?

THE TRANSFIGURATION

The Reading

Six days later, Jesus took with him Peter and James and his brother John and led them up a high mountain, by themselves. And he was transfigured before them, and his face shone like the sun, and his clothes became bright as light. Suddenly there appeared to them Moses and Elijah, talking with him. Then Peter said to Jesus, "Lord, it is good for us to be here; if you wish, I will set up three tents here, one for you, one for Moses, and one for Elijah." While he was still speaking, suddenly a bright cloud overshadowed them, and a voice from the cloud said, "This is my Son, the Beloved; with him I am well pleased; listen to him!" When the disciples heard this, they fell to the ground and were overcome by fear. But Jesus came and touched them, saying, "Get up and do not be afraid." And when they raised their eyes, they saw no one except Jesus himself alone.

As they were coming down the mountain, Jesus ordered

them, "Tell no one about the vision until after the Son of Man has been raised from the dead."

-Matthew 17:1–9

Through the Mystical Lens

The story of Jesus' Transfiguration is about change—not only the change the three witnesses see in Jesus, but their change and ours. On that mountain, the veil between heaven and earth lifts, and they glimpse what has always been true: God's glory shines through human flesh. The ordinary becomes radiant. Fear becomes awe. Vision becomes transformation.

I've experienced this same pattern in my own soul work with psychedelics. Like the disciples, I've been caught off guard by revelation. Sacred medicine dissolves the illusion of separation, opening me to the living truth that all creation is bound together in love. The curtain pulls back, and I see the same glory they saw—a world where everything belongs and nothing is wasted. But as with the Transfiguration, the experience isn't the goal. It's the beginning of integration—the work of living what we've seen.

Work with psychedelics and the Gospel share this in common: there is no escape from the body. The light of God doesn't rescue us from being human; it makes us *more* human. This deeper humanity—received through grace—is what we bring down the mountain, into our neighborhoods, our work, our relationships. Illumination is not meant to stay trapped in ecstasy or nostalgia but to be embodied in compassion, justice, and creativity.

When Jesus' friends fall in fear, he touches them and says, "Stand up. Don't be afraid." That same touch meets us after every revelation— when the glow fades and the real work begins. To stand up is to be resurrected, to live with open eyes and open hearts.

The Transfiguration, like a sacred psychedelic journey, reveals that love is the structure of reality. Integration is like resurrection—choosing to live in the power of new insight. We are changed by vision, yes, but even more by the courage to embody it: to walk back down the mountain and love the world as it is.

-The Rev. Dr. Paul D. Fromberg, Episcopal Church

Reflection Questions

1. Paul describes the Transfiguration as revealing "what has always been true: God's glory shines through human flesh." When have you suddenly recognized divine radiance in what you'd previously seen as ordinary? How did this shift in perception change your relationship to the material world?
2. The reflection emphasizes that "there is no escape from the body" and that divine light "makes us more human." How has your own mystical experience deepened rather than escaped your humanity? What does "deeper humanity" mean to you?
3. Paul writes that "integration is like resurrection." What vision or insight from your spiritual journey still awaits full embodiment? What keeps you from walking it down the mountain into daily life?

Spiritual Practice for the Week

This week, practice "Walking Down the Mountain":

Each morning, recall a moment of spiritual radiance: a time when you glimpsed the divine shining through ordinary reality. Hold this vision briefly, feeling its truth in your body.

Then ask: "How does this vision want to be lived today?" Listen for specific, embodied answers: a conversation to have, a kindness to offer, a justice to pursue.

Throughout your day, when you notice yourself longing for peak experience or spiritual escape, pause. Place your hand on your heart and remember: "The light doesn't rescue me from being human; it makes me more human."

Each evening, reflect: Where did I embody my vision today? Where did I resist coming down the mountain? No judgment, only noticing.

End the week by literally taking a walk, feeling your feet on the ground with each step. With every footfall, commit to one concrete way you'll live your transfiguration in the coming week.

Journal Prompts

Paul writes that after transfiguring experiences, "the glow fades and the real work begins." Describe a time when you had to integrate a profound spiritual insight into mundane reality. What was harder: receiving the vision or living it? How did the "real work" transform both you and the vision itself?

The reflection describes Jesus touching the fearful disciples, saying "Stand up. Don't be afraid." Write about a moment when divine touch helped you move from paralyzed awe into embodied action. What form did that touch take? What courage did it give you to love the world as it is?

PROPER 17 (PENTECOST 15): TAKE UP YOUR CROSS

The Reading

Jesus Foretells His Death and Resurrection

From that time on, Jesus began to show his disciples that he must go to Jerusalem and undergo great suffering at the hands of the elders and chief priests and scribes and be killed and on the third day be raised. And Peter took him aside and began to rebuke him, saying, "God forbid it, Lord! This must never happen to you." But he turned and said to Peter, "Get behind me, Satan! You are a hindrance to me, for you are setting your mind not on divine things but on human things."

The Cross and Self-Denial

Then Jesus told his disciples, "If any wish to come after me, let them deny themselves and take up their cross and follow me. For those who want to save their life will lose it, and those who lose their life for my sake will find it. For what will it profit them if they gain the whole world but forfeit their life? Or what will they give in return for their life?

"For the Son of Man is to come with his angels in the glory of his Father, and then he will repay everyone for what has been done. Truly I tell you, there are some standing here who will not taste death before they see the Son of Man coming in his kingdom."

-Matthew 16:21-28

Through the Mystical Lens

My father, a self-deputized grammar policeman, reminded me every Christmas season that the "is" in "Joy to the World, the Lord is Come" is a temporally special verb. In many consciousness-expanding experiences, time seems to fold in on itself. What has happened and what will happen are happening—now and forever. Birth, death, cross, resurrection, the coming of Christ-Consciousness: now, now, now.

You have heard it said, "Do not focus on the 'lower' worldly things, but rather on the 'higher' divine things." In different (non-normative) states of consciousness, personal preferential hierarchies and the urge to run toward the "pleasant" and away from the "painful" collapse into One Taste. Through the axis mundi Christ-energy, we realize the total saturation of the divine in and through humanity—in all its glorious, messy beauty.

In circles of shared expansive journeys, we sit together, taking up our crosses to feel each other's pain (have we not all tasted death?), holding it as our own, and calling in the kenotic strength of the Pain-Bearer. Space seems to shrink into one-pointed stillness.

One Cross. One Taste. One Love. One Heart.

-Rev. Brent Reynolds, Vine Contemplative Community + Tribe of the Open Heart

Reflection Questions

1. Brent describes time folding where "Birth, death, cross, resurrection" are happening "now, now, now." When have you experienced this collapse of linear time in spiritual practice, and how did it change your understanding of suffering and redemption?

2. The reflection speaks of hierarchies collapsing into "One Taste" where pleasant and painful merge. How does this non-dual awareness change your relationship to taking up your cross?

3. In circles of shared journey, participants "feel each other's pain...holding it as our own." When have you experienced personal suffering becoming universal, and universal suffering becoming personal?

Spiritual Practice for the Week

This week, practice "One Taste, One Cross":

Each morning, hold your hands in front of you, palms up. In your left hand, imagine holding something pleasant from your life. In your right, something painful. Feel both fully: their weight, texture, temperature.

Slowly bring your hands together until they meet at your heart. As they merge, breathe deeply and sense how both pleasant and painful are part of one life, one journey. Neither is rejected. Both are held.

Throughout the day, when you encounter suffering (yours or others'), pause and remember: "This is the One Cross we all carry." When you encounter joy, remember: "This is the One Love we all share."

Each evening, dedicate five minutes to feeling the world's pain as your own, your pain as the world's. Not to be overwhelmed, but to touch the truth that separation is illusion. End by resting in "One Heart": the Christ-consciousness that holds all.

Journal Prompts

Brent's father taught him about the "temporally special verb" where past/present/future collapse. Write about a moment in your spiritual journey when you experienced salvation, death, and resurrection not as sequential events but as simultaneous realities. How do you carry this knowing in ordinary time?

The reflection describes "calling in the kenotic strength of the Pain-Bearer" during collective healing work. Explore a time when bearing witness to another's pain, or having yours witnessed, transformed suffering into something sacred. What made this different from mere commiseration?

PROPER 18 (PENTECOST 16): TEACHINGS ON HUMILITY AND COMMUNITY

The Reading

True Greatness

At that time the disciples came to Jesus and asked, "Who is the greatest in the kingdom of heaven?" He called a child, whom he put among them, and said, "Truly I tell you, unless you change and become like children, you will never enter the kingdom of heaven. Whoever becomes humble like this child is the greatest in the kingdom of heaven. Whoever welcomes one such child in my name welcomes me.

The Parable of the Lost Sheep

"Take care that you do not despise one of these little ones, for I tell you, in heaven their angels continually see the face of my Father in heaven. What do you think? If a shepherd has a hundred sheep and one of them has gone astray, does he not leave the ninety-nine on the mountains and go in search of the one that went astray? And if he finds it, truly I tell you, he rejoices over it more than over the ninety-nine that never went astray. So it is not the will of your Father in heaven that one of these little ones should be lost.

Reproving Another Who Sins

"If your brother or sister sins against you, go and point out the fault when the two of you are alone. If you are listened to, you have regained that one. But if you are not listened to, take one or two others along with you, so that every word may be confirmed by the evidence of two or three witnesses. If that person refuses to listen to them, tell it to the church, and if the offender refuses to listen even to the church, let such a one be to you as a gentile and a tax collector. Truly I tell you, whatever you bind on earth will be bound in heaven, and whatever you loose on earth will be loosed in heaven. Again, truly I tell you, if two of you agree on earth about anything you ask, it will be done for you by my Father in heaven. For where two or three are gathered in my name, I am there among them."

-Matthew 18:1–5, 10–20

Through the Mystical Lens

Whatever you bind on earth, will be bound in heaven, and whatever you loose on earth, will be loosed in heaven. Let's be very clear: this earth, this time, this place is where the action is. However powerful, mystical, or ineffable our visions of other realms may be, our business is here on earth. Scrooge style. Whatever you see in a journey may not be an image of ultimate reality, but a reflection of the state of your soul now, an indication of what needs to be bound or loosed in your life. The intensity of our experience of the Divine does not excuse us from good discernment.

We set off on a journey to find the little ones, the lost sheep, the exiles whom the Father is not willing to see perish. We gain insights like, 'It turns out I'm not very good at this death-to-self thing; I let the wrong things die.' Good medicine doesn't leave us to our own devices. Through it, we learn how to nourish the precious child and the monsters within so that they don't go hungry and wreak havoc, but rather teach us how to play and praise. As within, so without. Our own exiles restored, we are freer to seek out people living on the margins and build community with them. You know, the old-timey church stuff that visionary experience should not distract us from, but prepare us for. I don't mean to overly functionalize our mysticism; I know why Peter said 'it's good to be on the mountain, let's build a tent and stay for a while.' It is good to be there. But 'they will know we are Christians by our love,' not our visions. Always back down the mountain we go on our journey to learn how good it is to be here, as well.

-The Rev. Megan Hollaway, Episcopal

Reflection Questions

1. Megan writes that visions may be "a reflection of the state of your soul now" rather than ultimate reality. How do you practice discernment between profound insight and personal projection in your mystical experiences?
2. The reflection speaks of nourishing "the precious child and the monsters within." Which inner exiles have you learned to feed rather than starve? How has this integration work changed your capacity to serve others?
3. "Always back down the mountain we go": when have you been tempted to build a tent and stay in the visionary realm? What called you back to earthly service, and what did you bring with you?

Spiritual Practice for the Week

This week, practice "Binding and Loosing on Earth":

Each morning, ask: "What needs to be bound in my life today? What needs to be loosed?" Be specific: perhaps binding a destructive pattern, loosing forgiveness, binding commitment to a practice, loosing rigid control.

Make one concrete earthly action based on your morning discernment. If you bound anxiety, take one step toward what you fear. If you loosed judgment, reach out to someone you've dismissed.

Throughout the day, when tempted to escape into spiritual abstraction, ask: "How does this insight want to be lived on earth?" Turn every elevation into grounding.

Each evening, examine: "How did I care for the little ones today, both within myself and in my community?" Notice without judgment. The work continues tomorrow.

End the week by identifying one marginalized part of yourself or your community that needs attention. Make a plan for concrete engagement.

Journal Prompts

Megan admits: "It turns out I'm not very good at this death-to-self thing; I let the wrong things die." Explore what you've mistakenly tried to kill in yourself: perhaps childlike wonder, healthy anger, or authentic needs. How are you learning to discern what should die versus what needs nourishing?

The reflection insists that mystical experience should prepare us for "old-timey church stuff": building community with those on the margins. Write about a time when a profound spiritual experience led you not to transcendence but to very earthly service. What was it like to discover heaven's work happens here?

PROPER 19 (PENTECOST 17): THE PARABLE OF THE UNFORGIVING SERVANT

The Reading

Forgiveness

Then Peter came and said to him, "Lord, if my brother or sister sins against me, how often should I forgive? As many as seven times?" Jesus said to him, "Not seven times, but, I tell you, seventy-seven times.

The Parable of the Unforgiving Servant

"For this reason the kingdom of heaven may be compared to a king who wished to settle accounts with his slaves. When he began the reckoning, one who owed him ten thousand talents was brought to him, and, as he could not pay, the lord ordered him to be sold, together with his wife and children and all his possessions and payment to be made. So the slave fell on his knees before him, saying, 'Have patience with me, and I will pay you everything.' And out of pity for him, the lord of that slave released him and forgave him the debt. But that same slave, as he went out, came upon one of his fellow slaves who owed him a hundred denarii, and seizing him by the throat he said, 'Pay what you owe.' Then his fellow slave fell down and pleaded with him, 'Have patience with me, and I will pay you.' But he refused; then he went and threw him into prison until he would pay the debt. When his fellow slaves saw what had happened, they were greatly distressed, and they went and reported to their lord all that had taken place. Then his lord summoned him and said to him, 'You wicked slave! I forgave you all that debt because you pleaded with me. Should you not have had mercy on your fellow slave, as I had mercy on you?' And in anger his lord handed him over to be tortured until he would pay his entire debt. So my heavenly Father will also do to every one of you, if you do not forgive your brother or sister from your heart."

-Matthew 18:21–35

Through the Mystical Lens

The Currency of Forgiveness.

"I came to make relatives", said Robert Two Bulls, a Lakota elder and Episcopal priest, to us who gathered at Pine Ridge Reservation. It struck a deep chord, causing me to wonder with whom I'm in relationship, and why.

In true relationship, there is no they or them. It's us. The phrase from the Lakota people, "Mitakuye Oyasin" means "all my relations," and is often said in prayer and ceremony, acknowledging that everything is related: people, animals, plants, and the mycelial network weaving beneath.

The mindset of empire is transactional, extractive, and self-serving. It leads to separateness, and emotional death. In the Kin-dom of God, kinship reigns supreme. All of creation is honored as an intimately connected family of things, woven together with love. And when you're family, you belong; and when you belong, you're welcomed and forgiven; and when you're welcomed and forgiven, you cannot help but keep that sacred medicine moving.

The young rabbi, a daring provocateur, tells a cautionary tale. What was that stingy man suffering from? Why did he do that? The separation he creates is hell, and a tortuous way to live. Forgiveness should flow in such abundance, that those multiples of seven that he talks about, flood the field with possibility. But doesn't unlimited forgiveness seem too lavish? Too expensive? Where's the return on my invested capital? If we have eyes to see, all those lucky sevens reveal the greatest treasure: the currency of God. The unforgiving servant took himself out of circulation, holding his money more tightly than the lives of others, even his own.

Forgiveness is the medicine that makes everything flow, and everyone rich. Not a debtor in sight. Born to cooperate and share, a divine altruism swims through us all. When times are hard, we bend toward each other, and tribal walls come down, as do the financial ledgers. The young teacher invites us to be a part of the Great Healing, the Great Forgiving. God help us, may we accept.

-Rev. James P. Marsh, Jr. (Jimmy), United Methodist Church

Reflection Questions

1. Jimmy quotes Robert Two Bulls: "I came to make relatives." How does viewing forgiveness as making relatives rather than settling accounts change your approach to those who've harmed you?
2. The reflection describes forgiveness as "the medicine that makes everything flow." When have you experienced

forgiveness—given or received—as medicine that restored circulation to what was blocked?

3. "In true relationship, there is no they or them. It's us." Where in your life do you still hold others as "them"? What would change if you recognized them as relatives?

Spiritual Practice for the Week

This week, practice "Making Relatives Through Forgiveness":

Each morning, bring to mind someone you consider "other": someone who owes you, who has harmed you, or whom you've written off. Hold them gently in awareness and whisper: "You are my relative."

Throughout the day, notice when you slip into transactional thinking: keeping score, calculating debts, measuring what others "owe" you. When this happens, pause and remember: "The currency of God is flowing through me."

Before any difficult interaction, silently acknowledge: "Mitakuye Oyasin—all my relations." Let this shift how you enter the conversation.

Each evening, practice one small act of forgiveness: releasing a grudge, letting go of a debt (emotional or literal), or simply blessing someone who irritated you. Feel how this act puts you back "in circulation."

Journal Prompts

Jimmy writes about "divine altruism" that "swims through us all." Describe a time when forgiveness arose in you not through effort but as a natural flow, when you discovered yourself already forgiving before you decided to forgive. What conditions allowed this grace to move through you?

The reflection warns that the unforgiving servant created "hell, and a tortuous way to live" through separation. Explore a time when withholding forgiveness tortured you more than the original wound. What finally freed you from this self-imposed prison? How did returning to circulation feel?

PROPER 20 (PENTECOST 18): THE LABORERS IN THE VINEYARD

The Reading

"For the kingdom of heaven is like a landowner who went out early in the morning to hire laborers for his vineyard. After agreeing with the laborers for a denarius for the day, he sent them into his vineyard. When he went out about nine o'clock, he saw others standing idle in the marketplace, and he said to them, 'You also go into the vineyard, and I will pay you whatever is right.' So they went. When he went out again about noon and about three o'clock, he did the same. And about five o'clock he went out and found others standing around, and he said to them, 'Why are you standing here idle all day?' They said to him, 'Because no one has hired us.' He said to them, 'You also go into the vineyard.' When evening came, the owner of the vineyard said to his manager, 'Call the laborers and give them their pay, beginning with the last and then going to the first.' When those hired about five o'clock came, each of them received a denarius. Now when the first came, they thought they would receive more; but each of them also received a denarius. And when they received it, they grumbled against the landowner, saying, 'These last worked only one hour, and you have made them equal to us who have borne the burden of the day and the scorching heat.' But he replied to one of them, 'Friend, I am doing you no wrong; did you not agree with me for a denarius? Take what belongs to you and go; I choose to give to this last the same as I give to you. Am I not allowed to do what I choose with what belongs to me? Or are you envious because I am generous?' So the last will be first, and the first will be last."

-Matthew 20:1–16

Through the Mystical Lens

"Take what belongs to you and go." We need explanations and excuses and reasons for what we have earned and have been given. Often, we feel ripped off or that what we earned is worth more than what we have received.

This story, though, is about the nature of heaven and our equal standing before God. We perceive heaven as something we achieve, something we deserve, something we have earned for work done. The gift of eternity we experience in our relationship with God is a mystical moment that extends through all of time. The gift of eternity can't be measured, earned, or given a value in payments or transactions. But since we perceive such a gift as payment for the work we have done, Jesus goes along with it for the sake of the parable.

Jesus explains that he is the one who decides who gets paid what, and since it is his money, he can choose what he does with it. The business of eternity, the work of heaven, pays out equally to all who are trying to earn their way, whether you worked the full day from early morning or for 20 minutes at the very end of the day. In the perspective of eternity, a lot of work or a little work looks like the same work, and therefore, work doesn't have much value relative to eternity. The fact of the matter, per Jesus, is that eternity, the kingdom of heaven, belongs to you, all of you in the same amount.

So take what belongs to you and go. There is no explanation, reason, or excuse that will measure the gift of eternity Jesus has provided. Yet the value of eternity is fully yours to take with you, whether you were there first or last. It is just that, if you were last, you know you deserve less. But even so, Jesus gives you just as much.

-Rev. Dr. Seth Jones, Congregational Church

Reflection Questions

1. Seth emphasizes that "the gift of eternity can't be measured, earned, or given a value in payments or transactions." When have you experienced grace that completely upended your sense of deserving? How did receiving what you hadn't earned change you?
2. The reflection notes that "in the perspective of eternity, a lot of work or a little work looks like the same work." How does this divine perspective challenge your attachment to spiritual accomplishment or comparison with others' journeys?
3. "If you were last, you know you deserve less. But even so, Jesus gives you just as much." When have you been the latecomer who received full blessing? How did this generosity toward you affect your view of divine justice?

Spiritual Practice for the Week

This week, practice "Taking What Is Yours":

Each morning, sit quietly and ask: "What truly belongs to me?" Not what I've earned, achieved, or accumulated, but what is mine in the economy of grace.

Throughout the day, notice when you're calculating spiritual worth: comparing your practice to others', measuring your "work" in prayer or service, feeling you deserve more or less than you receive. When this happens, pause and remember: "The gift of eternity belongs to me, fully, now."

Practice receiving one thing each day without earning it: a compliment, a kindness, a moment of beauty. Notice any discomfort with unearned gifts. Breathe and accept.

Each evening, place your hands over your heart and say: "I take what belongs to me: the full gift of divine love, no more and no less than anyone else receives." Rest in this radical equality.

Journal Prompts

Seth writes that Jesus "is the one who decides who gets paid what, and since it is his money, he can choose what he does with it." Explore your relationship with divine sovereignty. When have you grumbled against God's generosity toward others? What shifts when you recognize that grace isn't yours to distribute?

"Take what belongs to you and go." What would it mean to truly take the gift of eternity and go—to stop negotiating, comparing, or trying to earn more? Write about what you might do with your life if you fully believed you already possessed everything that matters.

PROPER 21 (PENTECOST 19): THE QUESTION OF AUTHORITY

The Reading

The Authority of Jesus Questioned

When he entered the temple, the chief priests and the elders of the people came to him as he was teaching and said, "By what authority are you doing these things, and who gave you this authority?" Jesus said to them, "I will also ask you one question; if you tell me the answer, then I will also tell you by what authority I do these things. Did the baptism of John come from heaven, or was it of human origin?" And they argued with one another, "If we say, 'From heaven,' he will say to us, 'Why, then, did you not believe him?' But if we say, 'Of human origin,' we are afraid of the crowd, for all regard John as a prophet." So they answered Jesus, "We do not know." And he said to them, "Neither will I tell you by what authority I am doing these things.

The Parable of the Two Sons

"What do you think? A man had two sons; he went to the first and said, 'Son, go and work in the vineyard today.' He answered, 'I will not,' but later he changed his mind and went. The father went to the second and said the same, and he answered, 'I go, sir,' but he did not go. Which of the two did the will of his father?" They said, "The first." Jesus said to them, "Truly I tell you, the tax collectors and the prostitutes are going into the kingdom of God ahead of you. For John came to you in the way of righteousness, and you did not believe him, but the tax collectors and the prostitutes believed him, and even after you saw it you did not change your minds and believe him.

-Matthew 21:23–32

Through the Mystical Lens

Let me invite you to take a moment and read this passage again. As you read, see if you can allow the story to read you, by taking note of the following two things, with a sense of openness, curiosity, and non-judgement:

a) Notice what happens in your body. Are there places of sensation or activation? Or not? Try to just notice the sensation, then see if you can notice any stories or meaning your mind wants to make of the sensation. Maybe notice if any judgements of others or yourself are present, without trying to fix or change anything.

b) Then ask yourself if there is any character in the story with whom you find yourself or identify. Try to avoid seeking or searching. Just allow what emerges to emerge.

Here is what happens to me. The first thing I notice is my relationship with authority, power, and control. The people in this passage want to know by what authority Jesus teaches and operates. I do the same thing. Even with these reflections, I am curious to read the bios of the contributors, to know where and how they were educated, what degrees they have, what places they have travelled, for how long have they been involved in their work. Curious, isn't it? I notice I want to hear the message, and something else in me also wants to know something about the credibility of the messenger.

Jesus does not play this game. I think Jesus' question about John the Baptist is just a cover. I marvel at Jesus' ability to mess with our egos and false need for certainty, for authority, for answers, for credibility, for safety, and control.

What is your relationship with power and authority?

What if the life and teaching of Jesus is an invitation... a strong, urgent invitation... to embark on a path away from the love of power, to the power of love?

What if love is not something for us to go out and find, to get, to earn, or to deserve?

What if instead, love is something each and every being in creation has?

What if spirituality is simply the experience of that re-connection with love in ourselves, with each other, and the cosmos?

What if love is an intelligence that seeks expression?

And what if love's expression is, as Richard Rohr writes, "always breaking out of the boxes we put it in?"

James Finley writes, "Love protects us from nothing even as it mysteriously sustains us in everything. And when love touches suffering, it turns the suffering into mercy."

Maybe these questions offer some insight into why the tax collectors, prostitutes, uneducated, inexperienced, irreligious, outcasts, non-Christians, the poor, the mystics, seem to get the power of love more than the religious power lovers?

I'm aware of a part of me that wants to use this story as a 'bomb' of sorts to lob back at the fundamentalist evangelical church I pastored. I'm aware of my default bias toward the educated and experienced people who teach and write about stuff like this. And, in this present moment, I'm aware of how this story pokes at my ego.

So now, I can receive this story with both laughter and sadness, with compassion, at the crazy manner The Way of love is unfolding in my life. In the last two years, I have experienced the death of my mother, the death of my father, a divorce, and getting fired from a job. And I have also experienced the welcoming of two new grandchildren, new connections with all three of my children (all very different), a new loving relationship, and a new role in shepherding a spiritual community in north Idaho after living in Seattle for 53 years.

I'm thinking of the words of one of my favorite hymns right now:

"Oh, to grace how great a debtor, daily I'm constrained to be. Let Thy goodness like a fetter, bind my wandering heart to Thee. Prone to wander, Lord I feel it, prone to leave the God I love. Here's my heart, Lord, take a seal it. Seal it for Thy courts above."

Amen, and so it is.

-James Kress, M.A., D.D. Senior Minister of Unity Center for Spiritual Growth

Reflection Questions

1. James asks: "What is your relationship with power and authority?" When have you found yourself needing credentials before receiving wisdom? What truth have you dismissed because the messenger lacked proper "authority"?
2. The reflection invites us to move "from the love of power, to the power of love." Where in your life are you still grasping

for control? What would it mean to let love's intelligence guide you instead?
3. James notes that "tax collectors, prostitutes...mystics, seem to get the power of love more than the religious power lovers." When has your own suffering or marginalization opened you to wisdom that privilege might have blocked?

Spiritual Practice for the Week

This week, practice "Authority of Love":

Begin each session by reading the passage slowly, then notice:

- Where do you feel activation in your body?
- What sensations arise without adding story or judgment?
- Which character draws you without searching or forcing?

Throughout the day, when you encounter someone teaching or sharing wisdom, notice your first impulse. Do you check their credentials? Judge their appearance? Assess their status?

Pause and ask instead: "What if love is speaking through this person?" Listen beneath qualifications to the intelligence of love seeking expression.

Each evening, reflect: Where did I choose the love of power today? Where did I choose the power of love? Hold both with the compassion James models: laughing at ego while grieving its grip.

Journal Prompts

James shares profound losses (parents' deaths, divorce, job loss) alongside new blessings (grandchildren, relationships, new role). Write about a time when life broke your boxes open: when authority and control crumbled but love remained to sustain you. How did suffering become mercy?

The reflection ends with "Prone to wander, Lord I feel it, prone to leave the God I love." Explore your own proneness to wander from love's authority back to ego's certainties. What fetter of goodness keeps drawing you home? What seal has been placed on your wandering heart?

PROPER 22 (PENTECOST 20): THE PARABLE OF THE WICKED TENANTS

The Reading

"Listen to another parable. There was a landowner who planted a vineyard, put a fence around it, dug a winepress in it, and built a watchtower. Then he leased it to tenants and went away. When the harvest time had come, he sent his slaves to the tenants to collect his produce. But the tenants seized his slaves and beat one, killed another, and stoned another. Again he sent other slaves, more than the first, and they treated them in the same way. Then he sent his son to them, saying, 'They will respect my son.' But when the tenants saw the son, they said to themselves, 'This is the heir; come, let us kill him and get his inheritance.' So they seized him, threw him out of the vineyard, and killed him. Now when the owner of the vineyard comes, what will he do to those tenants?" They said to him, "He will put those wretches to a miserable death and lease the vineyard to other tenants who will give him the produce at the harvest time."

Jesus said to them, "Have you never read in the scriptures:

'The stone that the builders rejected
    has become the cornerstone;
this was the Lord's doing,
    and it is amazing in our eyes'?
"Therefore I tell you, the kingdom of God will be taken away from you and given to a people that produces its fruits. The one who falls on this stone will be broken to pieces, and it will crush anyone on whom it falls."

When the chief priests and the Pharisees heard his parables, they realized that he was speaking about them. They wanted to arrest him, but they feared the crowds, because they regarded him as a prophet.

-Matthew 21:33–46

Through the Mystical Lens

"This is your brain on drugs," the old commercial warned, showing an egg frying in a pan. The parable of the vineyard reminds me of our government's War on Drugs which was a rejection of indigenous wisdom that plants are sacred messengers of the Divine. That television ad campaign shattered a deeper understanding that plant medicine, when approached with reverence, becomes a sacrament of remembrance that awakens the soul to its original harmony with God.

During a psilocybin journey, the ego is like the tenants of the vineyard as it begins to realize it is not the owner. It panics. It fights. It kills the messengers of truth that come in visions. The ego seeks control of the harvest, believing it can own the fruits of consciousness. But God, the true Landowner, has already planted a radiant intelligence within, brought to life by a network of mycelium that brings clarity.

As the psilocybin opens the mind, the walls of separation dissolve. The small mind, long trapped in its fenced vineyard of fear, is infused with divine light. Neural pathways awaken like vines in the sun, and perception becomes clearer. When the "son" arrives, the light of divine awareness, the ego's rebellion gives way to surrender. What seemed like death becomes rebirth, the cornerstone of a new consciousness.

The mind, now enlightened, becomes fertile soil for Spirit's vineyard. It sees through the illusion of ownership into the eternal unity of all life. The kingdom of God cannot be leased to the ego as it belongs to those who yield the harvest by letting go and allowing the sacred medicine to open the heart, revealing that the true wine of the soul has always been within.

-Rev. Dr. Cynthia Ramirez Lindenmeyer, Center for Spiritual Living

Reflection Questions

1. Cynthia describes the ego as "tenants" who panic when realizing they're not the owner. When have you experienced this recognition that you don't own or control the "vineyard" of your consciousness? How did your ego respond?
2. The reflection speaks of "messengers of truth that come in visions" being killed by the ego. What divine messages or insights have you resisted because they threatened your sense of control?
3. "What seemed like death becomes rebirth, the cornerstone of a new consciousness." How have your experiences of ego dissolution revealed themselves as foundation stones rather than destruction?

Spiritual Practice for the Week

This week, practice "Yielding the Vineyard":

Each morning, identify one area where you're grasping for control: a relationship, outcome, or aspect of yourself. Hold this awareness without judgment.

Sit quietly and visualize this area as a vineyard you've been trying to own. See yourself as a tenant, not the landlord. Breathe deeply and imagine opening the gates, inviting the true Owner to enter.

Throughout the day, when you catch yourself tightening control, pause. Place your hand on your heart and say: "This vineyard is not mine. I yield the harvest to Divine Intelligence."

Each evening, write one thing you released that day. Notice what grew in the space you created through surrender. Thank the true Landowner for tending what you cannot.

Journal Prompts

Cynthia connects the parable to "indigenous wisdom that plants are sacred messengers of the Divine." Explore your own relationship with consciousness-expanding experiences (whether through plants, meditation, or grace). When have these messengers arrived at your vineyard? How did you receive or reject them?

The reflection describes neural pathways awakening "like vines in the sun" as walls of separation dissolve. Write about a time when your "fenced vineyard of fear" opened to reveal the unity of all life. What walls came down? What connections were revealed? How do you tend this expanded awareness in daily life?

PROPER 23 (PENTECOST 21): THE PARABLE OF THE WEDDING BANQUET

The Reading

Once more Jesus spoke to them in parables, saying: "The kingdom of heaven may be compared to a king who gave a wedding banquet for his son. He sent his slaves to call those who had been invited to the wedding banquet, but they would not come. Again he sent other slaves, saying, 'Tell those who have been invited: Look, I have prepared my dinner, my oxen and my fat calves have been slaughtered, and everything is ready; come to the wedding banquet.' But they made light of it and went away, one to his farm, another to his business, while the rest seized his slaves, mistreated them, and killed them. The king was enraged. He sent his troops, destroyed those murderers, and burned their city. Then he said to his slaves, 'The wedding is ready, but those invited were not worthy. Go therefore into the main streets, and invite everyone you find to the wedding banquet.' Those slaves went out into the streets and gathered all whom they found, both good and bad, so the wedding hall was filled with guests.

"But when the king came in to see the guests, he noticed a man there who was not wearing a wedding robe, and he said to him, 'Friend, how did you get in here without a wedding robe?' And he was speechless. Then the king said to the attendants, 'Bind him hand and foot, and throw him into the outer darkness, where there will be weeping and gnashing of teeth.' For many are called, but few are chosen."

-Matthew 22:1–14

Through the Mystical Lens

This passage presents a tension. On the one hand, the Kingdom of Heaven and its healing are free and offered to all. Often, such universal gifts are undervalued. And so those initially offered the Kingdom not only "made light of it and went away" but seized, mistreated, and killed the messengers who delivered the news of the gift.

On the other hand, the Kingdom and its healing require investment and proper preparation. When the King offering these gifts responded to the rejection of his initial invitees by sending the messengers out in the streets to invite everyone, everyone came, even the uninvested and unprepared. That, too, sacrifices the gift.

Psychedelic medicine involves the same tension. Its experience and healing should be, in a sense, available to everyone. Hence, those to whom it has been most accessible often "make light of it," either using or dismissing it flippantly. In the latter case, it's not important. It's just what party animals do. And so they go "away, one to his farm, another to his business" or worse. In the former case, there's appreciation but no intentionality—no investment, no preparation, which has its own consequences. While truly horrific psychedelic experiences can be visited upon anyone without any discernible reason, such lack of intentionality is one way to increase the chances of being thrown "into the outer darkness."

-Bryan McCarthy, Roman Catholic Church

Reflection Questions

1. Bryan describes the tension between medicine being "available to everyone" yet requiring "investment and proper preparation." How do you hold both the democratic impulse to share healing widely and the need for sacred containment?
2. The reflection warns against treating medicine flippantly, whether through careless use or casual dismissal. Which of these dangers have you witnessed or experienced? What were the consequences?
3. The man without a wedding robe was speechless when confronted. When have you found yourself unprepared for a sacred encounter you thought you were ready for? What did that speechlessness teach you?

Spiritual Practice for the Week

This week, practice "Preparing Your Wedding Garment":

Each morning, ask yourself: "How am I preparing for sacred encounter today?" This might be formal spiritual practice, but also how you approach ordinary moments with intentionality.

Before any significant interaction: a difficult conversation, creative work, time in nature, pause and "put on your wedding robe." This means bringing your full presence, setting clear intention, and honoring the invitation you've received.

Notice when you're tempted to "make light of" sacred opportunities: rushing through prayer, half-listening to others, consuming experiences without digesting them. When you catch yourself, stop and choose: engage fully or step away until you can.

Each evening, review: Where did I show up "properly dressed" in consciousness today? Where did I arrive unprepared? No judgment, just noticing what level of preparation different encounters require.

Journal Prompts

Bryan notes that those initially offered the Kingdom "not only made light of it...but seized, mistreated, and killed the messengers." Reflect on a time when you or others rejected or attacked what was actually trying to heal or bless you. What fear or blindness caused this violent rejection of grace?

The reflection mentions that "truly horrific psychedelic experiences can be visited upon anyone without any discernible reason." Write about a difficult experience (psychedelic or otherwise) that came despite your best preparation. How did you make meaning from this seeming randomness? What role does mystery play in your spiritual understanding?

PROPER 24 (PENTECOST 22): THE QUESTION ABOUT PAYING TAXES

The Reading

Then the Pharisees went and plotted to entrap him in what he said. So they sent their disciples to him, along with the Herodians, saying, "Teacher, we know that you are sincere, and teach the way of God in accordance with truth, and show deference to no one, for you do not regard people with partiality. Tell us, then, what you think. Is it lawful to pay taxes to Caesar or not?" But Jesus, aware of their malice, said, "Why are you putting me to the test, you hypocrites? Show me the coin used for the tax." And they brought him a denarius. Then he said to them, "Whose head is this and whose title?" They answered, "Caesar's." Then he said to them, "Give therefore to Caesar the things that are Caesar's and to God the things that are God's." When they heard this, they were amazed, and they left him and went away.

-Matthew 22:15–22

Through the Mystical Lens

"Render unto Caesar" has always felt like a cosmic joke. Once Jesus adds "Render unto God what is God's" the joke comes full circle. It all belongs to whatever reality we define as God, source energy, overarching field of love. Unitarian Universalists are open to all kinds of names for the ultimate forces in the universe, but the oneness that comes with the Buddha's "loving kindness," and the ancient Hebrew command to "love your neighbor as yourself," the deal is pretty well sealed. Nothing doesn't belong to God. He/she/it owns the whole enchilada. And because there is only one divine energy, nobody is left out. Our morality becomes subject to the truth that we are all in this together. But Caesar is still standing there in ancient Palestine, much as tyrants still torture the poor and the dispossessed today. How do we render to that crowd when they so clearly reject love as the ultimate authority and work to draw unto themselves the coin of the realm and anything else they can get their hands on, including the blood and lives of those they rule?

Maybe one jewel of an answer can be found in the lives of Gandhi, Martin Luther King and others who have refused to buy civil authority that violates the rule of love. The immigration policies of the Trump administration have inspired civil disobedience in defiance of these abuses, physical violence and lawlessness. Are these protesters rendering unto Caesar? Maybe a broad interpretation would say "yes," because defiance, resistance, civil disobedience, all acts calling for justice, are all the earned renderings to these unjust Caesars. It's a shame that such defiance is necessary, but Jesus lived in a time when taxes were exacted at alarming, cruel rates, often at rates that left their victims with little to meet their other financial needs. It was cruelty beyond anything imagined by today's tax collectors. The tricksters who asked the question hoped to catch Jesus in an answer that would get him arrested or killed. Instead, Jesus gave them a cosmic joke. Everything belongs to God and sooner or later Caesar will live with the consequences of his cruelty. That ultimate fate has been rendered unto Caesar.

-Rev. Pat Jobe, Unitarian Universalist

Reflection Questions

1. Pat suggests that "defiance, resistance, civil disobedience, all acts calling for justice" might be what we properly render to unjust Caesars. When have you felt called to resist earthly authority in service of divine justice?
2. The reflection states "It all belongs to whatever reality we define as God" and "nobody is left out." How does this ultimate belonging inform your response to systems that exclude and oppress?
3. Jesus gave a "cosmic joke" that avoided the trap while revealing deeper truth. When have you navigated between complicity and martyrdom by finding a third way that exposed the absurdity of unjust power?

Spiritual Practice for the Week

This week, practice "Rendering Wisely":

Each morning, hold a coin in your hand. Feel its weight, temperature, edges. Ask: "What am I being asked to render today: to earthly powers, to divine justice, to my community?"

Throughout the day, notice where you automatically comply with "Caesar": systems, expectations, or authorities that may not align with love. Without judgment, simply observe: "I am rendering this. Is it mine to give?"

When you encounter injustice in the news, in your community, in your own life, pause and ask: "What does love require me to render here?" It might be protest, witness, resources, or strategic silence.

Each evening, examine: Where did I render to Caesar what belongs to God? Where did I withhold from love what love required? Offer both your compliance and resistance to divine wisdom.

Journal Prompts

Pat writes of protesters "rendering unto Caesar" through resistance, suggesting that "defiance...civil disobedience...are all the earned renderings to these unjust Caesars." Explore a time when you participated in or witnessed sacred resistance. How did opposing earthly authority become a form of spiritual practice?

The reflection ends with "sooner or later Caesar will live with the consequences of his cruelty." Write about your relationship to divine justice? Do you trust that oppressors face consequences? How does this belief (or struggle to believe) affect how you engage with injustice now?

PROPER 25 (PENTECOST 23): THE GREATEST COMMANDMENT

The Reading

The Greatest Commandment

When the Pharisees heard that he had silenced the Sadducees, they gathered together, and one of them, an expert in the law, asked him a question to test him. "Teacher, which commandment in the law is the greatest?" He said to him, " 'You shall love the Lord your God with all your heart and with all your soul and with all your mind.' This is the greatest and first commandment. And a second is like it: 'You shall love your neighbor as yourself.' On these two commandments hang all the Law and the Prophets."

The Question about David's Son

Now while the Pharisees were gathered together, Jesus asked them this question: "What do you think of the Messiah? Whose son is he?" They said to him, "The son of David." He said to them, "How is it then that David by the Spirit calls him Lord, saying,

> 'The Lord said to my Lord,
>   "Sit at my right hand,
>   until I put your enemies under your feet" '?
> "If David thus calls him Lord, how can he be his son?" No one
> was able to give him an answer, nor from that day did anyone
> dare to ask him any more questions.

-Matthew 22:34–46

Through the Mystical Lens

There are two "Greats" that are captured in the Gospels and they work symbiotically to bring balance and harmony to our spiritual walk. One is the Great Commandment and the second, is the Great Commission. My early years of ministry were utterly defined by a genuine yet somewhat rigid and zealous commitment to fulfill the Great Commission that Jesus left us. As someone who came to faith through a radical and dramatic Born-Again experience...one that catapulted me from a world of dysfunction into a discipline-oriented (a necessary foundation for my own spiritual journey) understanding of my role as a new believer, the Great Commission was a concrete outlet for my zeal and gratitude. That zeal led my family and I to pour our lives into ministry in marginalized communities all around the world, and is a fire that still burns bright. But it wasn't until I had my first experiences with psilocybin during the Religious Professional Study with Johns Hopkins and NYU, which I also would describe as a Born-Again experience, that I was able to more fully grasp the importance of The Great Commandment and how necessary it is to hold both of these "Greats" in tension.

In the Great Commandment, Jesus addresses the religious scholars of his day in Jerusalem on the week he would be betrayed and crucified, having just marched into town on a donkey to shouts of Hosanna, and headed straight to the Temple to throw down the gauntlet on the religious exploitation that had become the norm. To further ruffle theological feathers, Jesus synthesized all the teachings of the Law and the Prophets into what he describes into a 1, 2 punch that can only be described as the GREATEST Commandment in the Scriptures: Love God, Love your neighbor, Love Yourself. This is a great triad of Love, and although is sound like an over simplification of all of the Scriptures, it takes a lifetime to discover the depth of faith and commitment it takes to live a simple life defined by a Love for God, Loving those around us, and Lovingly accepting all of the unchangeables that define who we are.

-Rev. Ruben Nuño, Church of the Living Hope, UCC

Reflection Questions

1. Ruben asks about aspects of faith that "God might be wanting to simplify." What religious complexity have you added to your spiritual life that obscures rather than reveals love? What would stripping it back to essentials look like?
2. The reflection describes holding "greats" in tension— particularly the Great Commission and Great Commandment. Where in your spiritual life have you emphasized doing over being, or action over love? How might these rebalance?
3. Ruben mentions his psilocybin experience as a "Born-Again experience" that helped him grasp the Great Commandment. When has a mystical encounter simplified rather than complicated your faith? What essential truth emerged?

Spiritual Practice for the Week

This week, practice "Living the Triad of Love":

Each morning: Hold these three movements in your awareness: Love of God, Love of Neighbor, Love of Self. Notice which feels most accessible today and begin there.

Monday & Tuesday: Focus on loving God with your whole being. This might mean ecstatic worship, silent contemplation, or simply moving through your day with constant awareness of divine presence. Let yourself be unselfconscious in your devotion.

Wednesday & Thursday: Turn toward loving your neighbor. Look for one unexpected opportunity each day to bless someone without calculation or need for thanks. Let love move through you spontaneously.

Friday & Saturday: Practice radical self-love. Honor your journey, tend your needs, celebrate your growth. This isn't indulgence but recognition of yourself as beloved.

Sunday: Rest in the awareness that these three loves are actually one movement. Notice how loving God opens you to love others; how loving others teaches you to love yourself; how self-love frees you to love God more fully.

Journal Prompts

Ruben shares how his psilocybin experience helped him "more fully grasp the importance of The Great Commandment" after years focused on the Great Commission. Write about a time when mystical experience rebalanced your spiritual life. What had become overemphasized? What essential element had been neglected? How did the rebalancing feel in your body and daily practice?

The reflection describes the Great Commandment as taking "a lifetime to discover the depth of faith and commitment it takes to live a simple life defined by" love. Choose the aspect of the triad that challenges you most: loving God, neighbor, or self. Write honestly about why this particular love is difficult for you. What would change if you could receive and give this love more freely?

PROPER 26 (PENTECOST 24): THE DENUNCIATION OF THE SCRIBES AND PHARISEES

The Reading

Then Jesus said to the crowds and to his disciples, "The scribes and the Pharisees sit on Moses's seat; therefore, do whatever they teach you and follow it, but do not do as they do, for they do not practice what they teach. They tie up heavy burdens, hard to bear, and lay them on the shoulders of others, but they themselves are unwilling to lift a finger to move them. They do all their deeds to be seen by others, for they make their phylacteries broad and their fringes long. They love to have the place of honor at banquets and the best seats in the synagogues and to be greeted with respect in the marketplaces and to have people call them rabbi. But you are not to be called rabbi, for you have one teacher, and you are all brothers and sisters. And call no one your father on earth, for you have one Father, the one in heaven. Nor are you to be called instructors, for you have one instructor, the Messiah. The greatest among you will be your servant. All who exalt themselves will be humbled, and all who humble themselves will be exalted.

-Matthew 23:1–12

Through the Mystical Lens

"The greatest among you will be your servant."

When I tell people I'm a retired United Methodist pastor, they're often surprised. Sometimes they even look a little startled. I think it's because I don't fit the image they have of a "Christian leader." More than once, someone has said, "You don't seem like a preacher." Usually, they mean it as a compliment—they find me open, curious, and nonjudgmental. But underneath that is a kind of sadness. Their encounters with Christians have often left them feeling judged, not loved.

Jesus saw the same thing in his day. The religious leaders—the Pharisees and scribes—were supposed to help people draw near to God, but instead they made faith feel heavy and exclusive. Jesus didn't hold back. He told them their pride and love of titles kept others from experiencing the very God they claimed to serve.

That stings a little, especially for those of us who've spent our lives in ministry. We write devotionals like this one and then include a bio at the end, listing our degrees and titles. We want to build trust, but there's irony there. Jesus reminds us that there's only one true teacher, and we're all brothers and sisters. We all share the same Spirit, the same divine breath.

In sacred medicine circles, people sometimes talk about "ego dissolution"—a deep sense of oneness with the earth and with each other. That experience mirrors what Jesus was teaching: real spirituality isn't about hierarchy. It's about humility, connection, and love.

When we lead with love, we lift burdens instead of adding them. Maybe the best credential any of us can claim is a humble heart.

Prayer:

Loving God, free me from the need to be important or admired. Keep me grounded in your love and open to the wisdom of others. Help me to listen well, serve joyfully, and see your image in everyone I meet. Amen.

-Rev. Betsy Ouellette Zierden, United Methodist

Reflection Questions

1. The reflection mentions "ego dissolution, a deep sense of oneness with the earth and with each other" as mirroring Jesus's teaching. When have you experienced this dissolution of hierarchy and separation in your own mystical journey? How does remembering that oneness affect how you relate to spiritual authorities or teachers?

2. "Their encounters with Christians have often left them feeling judged, not loved." After experiencing unconditional love in expanded states, how do you navigate religious communities that may still operate from judgment? What helps you stay connected to faith traditions while holding space for their human limitations?

3. Betsy suggests "the best credential any of us can claim is a humble heart." How has your spiritual journey transformed your understanding of spiritual authority? What wisdom have you gained about when to teach and when to simply serve?

Spiritual Practice for the Week

Each day this week, practice "credential releasing." Begin your morning by sitting quietly and bringing to mind any titles, achievements, or spiritual experiences you use to establish your worth or authority. Hold them gently, acknowledging their place in your journey.

Then consciously set them aside. For the next five minutes, rest in the simple truth that you are a sibling among siblings, sharing the same divine breath. Throughout your day, when you notice yourself reaching for credentials (mental or actual) to validate your perspective, pause. Ask yourself: "How can I serve in this moment without needing to be seen as special?"

Before bed, reflect on moments when you connected with others from this place of shared humanity rather than hierarchy. Notice how different it feels to relate as equals under one Teacher.

Journal Prompts

Betsy shares how people say "You don't seem like a preacher" as a compliment, finding them "open, curious, and nonjudgmental." Write about a time when your expanded consciousness experiences made you "not seem like" what people expected of a Christian. How do you hold both your faith identity and your broader spiritual understanding?

"We want to build trust, but there's irony there," the reflection notes about listing credentials even while teaching humility. Explore your own relationship with spiritual credentials or experiences. When do you find yourself wanting to establish your authority through what you've seen or learned? How can you share wisdom while remaining a fellow traveler rather than an elevated teacher?

PROPER 27 (PENTECOST 25): THE PARABLE OF THE TEN BRIDESMAIDS

The Reading

"Then the kingdom of heaven will be like this. Ten young women took their lamps and went to meet the bridegroom. Five of them were foolish, and five were wise. When the foolish took their lamps, they took no oil with them, but the wise took flasks of oil with their lamps. As the bridegroom was delayed, all of them became drowsy and slept. But at midnight there was a shout, 'Look! Here is the bridegroom! Come out to meet him.' Then all those young women got up and trimmed their lamps. The foolish said to the wise, 'Give us some of your oil, for our lamps are going out.' But the wise replied, 'No! there will not be enough for you and for us; you had better go to the dealers and buy some for yourselves.' And while they went to buy it, the bridegroom came, and those who were ready went with him into the wedding banquet, and the door was shut. Later the other young women came also, saying, 'Lord, lord, open to us.' But he replied, 'Truly I tell you,

I do not know you.' Keep awake, therefore, for you know neither the day nor the hour.

-Matthew 25:1–13

Through the Mystical Lens

There's a wedding somewhere in the dark, a bridegroom running late, and ten young women with lamps trying to hold the in-between. It feels familiar—promise made, party coming, and yet time stretches longer than anyone thought it would.

All of them get drowsy. All of them fall asleep. No shame in that. Bodies have limits. The parable refuses the hustle. The crisis doesn't arrive until the shout, until the moment asks for light you either have or you don't.

Oil is the quiet center of the story. Not drama, not fear—oil. It isn't spectacle; it's supply. In the ancient world, you didn't magic oil out of the air at midnight. You had what you had because you'd tended something earlier—pressed olives, filled flasks, kept a reserve.

There are parts of faith you simply can't borrow. No one can hand you a practiced tenderness for the poor at the last second. No one can loan you a life of prayer when panic hits. No one can transfer a rooted, non-anxious presence into your hands when the room goes dark. Those are grown over time—everyday yeses, a thousand small refusals, the long work of becoming congruent with Love.

And still, this is not a parable about earning. It's about capacity. The wise aren't better people; they are people who expected delay and made room for it. Oil looks like habits that hold when the clock slips —Scripture that has worn a path through the heart, Sabbath that loosens the tyranny of urgency, generosity that refuses wealth's spell, friendships that tell the truth and stay.

For some, awakening has come in one bright rush—consciousness widened, life shimmering. Beautiful. Keep the awe. And let it ferment into oil—integrated, steady light for long nights and late arrivals.

At midnight the shout goes up, and what we've cultivated burns. Not to impress a gatekeeper, but to move with joy into what we were made for: the feast. Lamps trimmed. Flames steady. Oil enough to cross the threshold.

-Rev. Dr. Andrea F. Smith, United Methodist

Reflection Questions

1. Andrea writes: "There are parts of faith you simply can't borrow." What spiritual capacities have you discovered must be cultivated personally and cannot be transferred, even by well-meaning friends?
2. The reflection distinguishes between "earning" and "capacity"—the wise weren't better, just prepared for delay. Where in your spiritual life have you learned to expect delays and make room for them?
3. "For some, awakening has come in one bright rush...let it ferment into oil." If you've experienced sudden spiritual opening, how are you allowing it to ferment into steady, sustainable light?

Spiritual Practice for the Week

This week, practice "Tending Your Oil":

Each morning, check your spiritual oil level. What reserves do you have for unexpected demands? Don't judge, just notice. Are you running on fumes or do you have depth to draw from?

Choose one "oil-building" practice to strengthen this week:

- Scripture memorization (letting words wear paths in your heart)
- Sabbath moments (refusing urgency's tyranny)
- Acts of generosity (breaking wealth's spell)
- Truth-telling conversation (deepening authentic connection)

When you feel depleted or panicked, resist the urge to borrow others' spiritual reserves. Instead, return to your own practices, even if they feel small. Trust what you've been cultivating.

Before sleep, appreciate whatever oil you've tended today; even a teaspoon counts. This isn't about perfection but about steady, patient preparation for whenever the Bridegroom arrives.

Journal Prompts

Andrea lists specific forms of oil: "Scripture that has worn a path through the heart, Sabbath that loosens the tyranny of urgency, generosity that refuses wealth's spell." Which of these reserves are strong in your life? Which flasks need refilling? Write about one practice you want to deepen.

The reflection notes that "all of them get drowsy. All of them fall asleep. No shame in that." Write about a time when you felt ashamed of your spiritual drowsiness or limitations. How might this parable's compassion for human limits change your relationship to your own capacity?

PROPER 28 (PENTECOST 26): THE PARABLE OF THE TALENTS

The Reading

"For it is as if a man, going on a journey, summoned his slaves and entrusted his property to them; to one he gave five talents, to another two, to another one, to each according to his ability. Then he went away. At once the one who had received the five talents went off and traded with them and made five more talents. In the same way, the one who had the two talents made two more talents. But the one who had received the one talent went off and dug a hole in the ground and hid his master's money. After a long time the master of those slaves came and settled accounts with them. Then the one who had received the five talents came forward, bringing five more talents, saying, 'Master, you handed over to me five talents; see, I have made five more talents.' His master said to him, 'Well done, good and trustworthy slave; you have been trustworthy in a few things; I will put you in charge of many things; enter into the joy of your master.' And the one with the two talents also came forward, saying, 'Master, you handed over to me two talents; see, I have made two more talents.' His master said to him, 'Well done, good and trustworthy slave; you have been trustworthy in a few things; I will put you in charge of many things; enter into the joy of your master.' Then the one who had received the one talent also came forward, saying, 'Master, I knew that you were a harsh man, reaping where you did not sow and gathering where you did not scatter, so I was afraid, and I went and hid your talent in the ground. Here you have what is yours.' But his master replied, 'You wicked and lazy slave! You knew, did you, that I reap where I did not sow and gather where I did not scatter? Then you ought to have invested my money with the bankers, and on my return I would have received what was my own with interest. So take the talent from him, and give it to the one with the ten talents. For to all those who have, more will be given, and they will have an abundance, but from those who have nothing, even what they have will be taken away. As for this worthless slave, throw him into the outer darkness, where there will be weeping and gnashing of teeth.'

-Matthew 25:14–30

Through the Mystical Lens

"A man, going on a journey, summoned his slaves…"

Joanna cleared her throat.

"Jesus," she interrupted. He paused and smiled, knowing that Joanna's wisdom was worth listening to.

Others in the group leaned forward to hear her.

"The man going on the journey summoned his slaves," she continued. "I'm not sure where you're headed with this story, but, slavery! I admit, it's taken me too long to come to this conclusion, but slavery as an institution is unjust! Why does any person think that 'owning' another person and their labor is in any way fair or just?"

Jesus nodded thoughtfully. "I'll admit," he said, "That's not where I was headed with this story. I was thinking about a tale of slaves using their talents wisely. But you're taking this in a different direction."

"I want to talk about using talents wisely, for sure," she replied. "But what if our underlying assumptions are faulty? What if things like slavery and economic injustice and militarism are so baked into our thinking that we only tell surface stories and don't dig deeper to address greater problems.'

Other disciples murmured affirmations.

One of the group, Bartholomew, who had been resting his head in the lap of his boyfriend Thaddeus, sat up, "Or patriarchy or homophobia? Joanna, we talk about it all the time. Everyone refers to you as 'Joanna, wife of Chuza.' Chuza is a great guy. But you're you, apart from who your spouse is. And Thaddeus and me," he reached for the hand of his partner of many years, "People ignore us or belittle us or threaten us."

Joanna winked at Bartholemew in a way that said, "I see you, I hear you, I affirm you."

"That's why I value being part of this group," Jesus said. "You help me think about things in new ways. We learn and grow together. We integrate our wisdom."

Jesus paused and looked at the olive trees growing on the hillside around them. "I started this parable saying a man was going on a journey...' It's me! I'm the person on a journey. I'm changing. We are all. Life is a trip, an adventure, a journey."

-Rev. Dr. Timothy Tutt, United Church of Christ

Reflection Questions

1. In the reimagined dialogue, Jesus says "Life is a trip, an adventure, a journey" and acknowledges he's changing. After your own consciousness-expanding experiences, how have you discovered that even your understanding of sacred texts continues to evolve? What gifts or "talents" from your journey are you still learning to integrate?

2. Joanna interrupts Jesus to challenge the parable's assumptions, and he welcomes her wisdom. When has your expanded awareness led you to question traditional religious teachings? How do you balance honoring scripture while also trusting your direct spiritual knowing?

3. The original parable speaks of hiding talents in fear versus investing them boldly. What spiritual gifts or insights from your mystical experiences have you "buried" out of fear of judgment? What would it look like to invest these talents courageously in service of love?

Spiritual Practice for the Week

This week, practice "collaborative wisdom meditation" inspired by the reflection's image of Jesus learning from his friends. Each day, bring one insight from your spiritual journey into dialogue with scripture or tradition.

Sit quietly and recall a truth you've discovered through expanded consciousness. Then open your Bible or recall a traditional teaching. Instead of forcing agreement or choosing sides, let them converse. What does your experience teach the tradition? What does tradition offer your experience?

Notice when you want to bury your knowing out of fear (like the one-talent servant) versus when you feel called to share it boldly. End each session by asking: "How can I invest this integrated wisdom in service of collective awakening?"

Journal Prompts

The reflection shows Jesus saying "That's not where I was headed with this story" when Joanna redirects the conversation. Write about a time when your spiritual journey took you somewhere completely unexpected from where you thought you were headed. How did you learn to trust the redirection?

"We learn and grow together. We integrate our wisdom," Jesus says in the reimagined scene, after declaring "It's me! I'm the person on a journey." Write about how recognizing yourself as the one on the journey has changed your relationship to spiritual teachings. How do your mystical experiences reveal that everything, even scripture, is ultimately about your own learning, healing, and growing? Who helps you integrate this wisdom?

PROPER 29 (PENTECOST 27 / CHRIST THE KING/REIGN OF CHRIST): THE JUDGMENT OF THE NATIONS

The Reading

"When the Son of Man comes in his glory and all the angels with him, then he will sit on the throne of his glory. All the nations will be gathered before him, and he will separate people one from another as a shepherd separates the sheep from the goats, and he will put the sheep at his right hand and the goats at the left. Then the king will say to those at his right hand, 'Come, you who are blessed by my Father, inherit the kingdom prepared for you from the foundation of the world, for I was hungry and you gave me food, I was thirsty and you gave me something to drink, I was a stranger and you welcomed me, I was naked and you gave me clothing, I was sick and you took care of me, I was in prison and you visited me.' Then the righteous will answer him, 'Lord, when was it that we saw you hungry and gave you food or thirsty and gave you something to drink? And when was it that we saw you a stranger and welcomed you or naked and gave you clothing? And when was it that we saw you sick or in prison and visited you?' And the king will answer them, 'Truly I tell you, just as you did it to one of the least of these brothers and sisters of mine, you did it to me.' Then he will say to those at his left hand, 'You who are accursed, depart from me into the eternal fire prepared for the devil and his angels, for I was hungry and you gave me no food, I was thirsty and you gave me nothing to drink, I was a stranger and you did not welcome me, naked and you did not give me clothing, sick and in prison and you did not visit me.' Then they also will answer, 'Lord, when was it that we saw you hungry or thirsty or a stranger or naked or sick or in prison and did not take care of you?' Then he will answer them, 'Truly I tell you, just as you did not do it to one of the least of these, you did not do it to me.' And these will go away into eternal punishment but the righteous into eternal life."

-Matthew 25:31–46

Through the Mystical Lens

Wow, what a passage for this day and age! The coming of a king, the judgment of people as sheep or goats, with blessings for those who showed compassion and helped their fellow human beings. Seems to be a pretty solid scriptural rebuttal to the idea of "toxic empathy."

The biblical directives are pretty clear. Feed the hungry, give water to the thirsty, take care of the sick, clothe the naked, and welcome the stranger. These are who will "inherit the kingdom of God." Promises of kingly rewards aside, why does the world seem to be getting this so wrong right now?

Someday Scripture predicts, when "the Son of Man comes in glory," things will be made clear and we will finally recognize Christ where Christ has always been: in the face of the hungry, the forgotten, the vulnerable, the unprotected. Christ is not merely *represented* in the poor; Christ *is* the poor. Christ *is* the naked, the hungry. The imprisoned one *is* the Incarnation.

But perhaps this is not some far off event. Perhaps this is a sort of mystical awakening. Maybe it's up to us to notice when God shows up. We can see the kingdom here and now. We can see the coming of Christ here and now. This is recognition by awakening. When we recognize Christ and the ego falls away, compassion is not an effort; it is the only thing left. When we recognize Christ then serving the sick, the poor, and the naked isn't about sacrificing resources or saving our own skins, it's about being who we were meant to be.

The sheep are those who have begun to see from unity instead of separation, those who no longer meet another as an "other." The goats are not evil people, but those who can't yet see Christ: the part of us still caught in illusion, still protecting itself, still hurting.

The moment the veil lifts, the moment we see Christ we don't discover a distant throne, we discover the radiance of God woven into the very people we were trained by the world not to see.

The Kingdom is not something we inherit *later*; it is the dimension we awaken into when love becomes our way of seeing.

-Rev. B. Jeffrey Vidt, United Church of Christ

Reflection Questions

1. Jeffrey asks about experiencing "sudden recognition" of someone's sacredness. When have you looked at someone society devalues and suddenly seen divine radiance? What dissolved that allowed this seeing?
2. The reflection suggests that "compassion is not an effort; it is the only thing left" when the ego falls away. When have you experienced compassion arising naturally rather than through moral effort?

3. How might viewing separation between "helper" and "helped" as illusion transform your approach to service? What changes when you see giving and receiving as one movement?

Spiritual Practice for the Week

This week, practice "Here is Christ":

Throughout each day, when you encounter anyone: family, strangers, those asking for help, those in positions of power, pause internally and acknowledge: "Here is Christ."

Set aside 10 minutes each evening to review your day's encounters. Bring each person to mind, from the grocery clerk to the difficult colleague to anyone you avoided. With each face, breathe slowly and repeat: "Here is Christ."

Notice:

- Where was this recognition easy? Where was it nearly impossible?
- How did this lens change your interactions?
- What resistance arose to seeing certain people as Christ?

Don't force feelings of reverence. Simply practice the seeing. Let the recognition work on you in its own way.

Journal Prompts

Jeffrey writes that "Christ is not merely represented in the poor; Christ IS the poor." Describe a moment when you encountered the holy precisely in vulnerability, yours or another's. How did recognizing divinity in weakness rather than strength reorganize your spiritual understanding?

The reflection reframes judgment: "The goats are not evil people, but those who can't yet see." Explore a time when your own inability to see another's sacredness caused harm. What veil had to lift for recognition to dawn? How do you hold compassion for the parts of yourself still learning to see?

ABOUT THE CONTRIBUTORS

DR. JAMIE BEACHY

Dr. Jamie Beachy was raised in the Mennonite tradition and now practices chaplaincy in an inter-religious capacity. Her commitment to chaplaincy advances ethics rooted in eco-spirituality. Jamie was a sub-investigator for MAPS Phase 3 clinical trials in Boulder, Colorado, researching the safety and efficacy of MDMA-assisted therapy for the treatment of PTSD and she was approved as a consultant supervisor, offering consultation for practitioners training in MDMA-Assisted therapy. Jamie was Faculty Co-founder of Naropa University's Center for Psychedelic Studies and co-founded the Psychedelic Care Research Network through the Transforming Chaplaincy initiative. She now serves as a Field Scholar with the Emory Center for Psychedelics and Spirituality and is the current Chair of the Board of Directors of the Chacruna Institute for Psychedelic Plant Medicines. Jamie seeks to bring insights from professional spiritual health to the field of psychedelic studies and psychedelic-assisted therapy.

KERRA BECKER ENGLISH

Perpetual curiosity drives Rev. Kerra Becker English's engagement with scriptural interpretation. She prefers to preach and teach from the questions, not the answers. As a spiritual companion, she guides others through deep listening and with the occasional hearty laugh. Her wealth of experience as a pastor (Presbyterian) and spiritual guide has led her to write a field guide to the inner journey called, "True Awakening: The Highs, Lows, and Mess of Spiritual Transformation." She believes the spiritual journey will always be sparked by curiosity and grounded in love.

THOM BELOTE

Thom lives in Chapel Hill, NC, and has been the minister of The Community Church of Chapel Hill, Unitarian Universalist, since 2014. He holds degrees from Harvard Divinity School and Reed College. He is drawn towards learning about and thinking about mystical and paranormal experiences.

WENDY CLIFF

Wendy D. Cliff is an Episcopal priest and interfaith chaplain who loves interfaith dialogue, trauma-care, good food, stories, ancient trees, ritual, and paper arts. A graduate of UC Berkeley's Center for the Science of Psychedelics facilitator training program and Seminary of the Wild's Eco-Spiritual Direction training program, she supports folks seeking to live out their spiritual values in new ways, especially during this chaotic time in history. She offers group spiritual direction through Ligare and also meets with individuals on the land or online. She lives in Bend, Oregon where Measure 109 made it the first state to legalize a regulated program for accessing psilocybin care in safe and supportive settings.

JESSICA FELIX ROMERO

Dr. Jessica Felix Romero is a national faith leader advancing progressive religious movement building, interspiritual collaboration, and theological innovation. With over 15 years of experience in social justice advocacy, organizing, and communications, she previously served as Vice President and Chief Strategy and Impact Officer at Sojourners, where she helped set faith-based narrative change and justice-oriented policy agendas. She currently serves as the board chair for Ligare. Holding a doctorate in conflict analysis and resolution, Jessica integrates holistic systems thinking with transformative design to foster social change. Her work explores the intersections of spirituality, ancestral wisdom, and Christianity. Her latest publication, God's Wisdom Implanted in All Things (2024), examines entheogenic plant wisdom, Christian mysticism, and embodied theology as pathways to emergent wisdom. A student of somatic writing and embodied leadership, Jessica is committed to reclaiming ancient spiritual traditions for contemporary faith communities.

PAUL FROMBERG

The Rev. Dr. Paul Fromberg is the rector of St. Gregory of Nyssa Episcopal Church. Paul is an iconographer and has practiced for over 20 years. In addition to his congregational ministry, Paul has served as an adjunct faculty member at the Church Divinity School of the Pacific. His research interests include the phenomenon of transformation, particularly in relation to the experiences of beauty, social engagement and friendship. The intersection of art, liturgy, and devotional practice. Iconography and iconology. Liturgy and ritual in expanded states of consciousness. He is the author of *The Art of Transformation* (Church Publishing, 2017) and *The Art of Disruption* (Seabury Books, 2021). Paul is married to Grant Martin and lives in San Francisco with their dog, Miles.

MEGAN HOLLAWAY

The Rev. Megan Hollaway is an Episcopal priest, clinical social worker, and spiritual director. She is the Director of Education at Ligare, a Christian psychedelic society, and provides psychedelic chaplaincy in the context of state-legal retreats and integration support. She is a graduate of Yale Divinity School, and completed psychedelic-assisted facilitator training at UC Berkeley's Center for the Science of Psychedelics and at the CIIS Center for Psychedelic Therapy and Research. Deeply formed by Benedictine spirituality, she integrates wisdom from the Desert Fathers and monastic traditions with contemporary insights from therapeutic, somatic, and nature-based practices.

DOUG HOOVER

Doug is a retired U.S. Army chaplain, retired ordained Presbyterian minister, and current Licensed Marriage and Family Therapist. He holds a Doctor of Ministry degree and has advanced clinical training in trauma and relationship therapies. Doug continues to serve active-duty service members and veterans through his private practice in Southern Pines, North Carolina. He also enjoys helping others process healing and integrate spiritually significant experiences into their lives, something that often happens after they attend healing plant medicine retreats. Doug and his wife, Kathy, enjoy the outdoors and spending time with their children and grandchildren.

PAT JOBE

Pat Jobe is the minister of the Unitarians of Lake Norman and All Souls Community in Rutherford County, both in North Carolina. He was arrested twice protesting the refusal of the S.C. legislature to extend Medicaid benefits. He writes for a local paper in his hometown of Forest City. For 19 years, he and co-writers have performed Radio Free Bubba on WNCW.org. He loves his wife, Gabriele, his family and his dogs and everything. His favorite words found on the back of a car are, "Life is good." He can be found on Facebook. He's the one with the picture of him kissing his two-year-old granddaughter. He has been a pastoral minister for 32 years. He is the author of 365 Ways To Criticize The Preacher and other books.

SETH D. JONES

Reverend Dr. Seth Jones is a Spiritual and Grief Counselor in La Crosse, WI. He has had a circuitous path through the spiritual landscape, including a Master of Arts in Religious Studies, which focused on the Gnostics. He lived in a new age martial arts commune for 8 years. Seth has studied Tai Chi Chuan for 35 years. He received his Masters of Divinity degree from Luther Seminary in St. Paul, MN. For 15 years, Rev. Dr. Jones pastored Congregational churches in Yellowstone National Park and Midcoast Maine. He was a participant in the Religious Leaders Study with Johns Hopkins Consciousness and Psychedelic Lab in December 2018. As a result of his experiences, he went back to school and received a Doctor of Ministry in Extraordinary Spiritual Experiences from Portland Seminary in Portland, OR. His work in Extraordinary Spiritual Experiences comes from many decades studying and researching strange, unusual, weird, and bizarre stories, as well as his own mystical encounters and experiences.

JAMES KRESS

James Kress is a father of three amazing grown children and proud grandfather of two grandsons and a granddaughter. He is the oldest of five brothers, and a stepson. He was born in Milwaukee, Wisconsin, and lived 53 years in the eastern suburbs of Seattle, Washington. He has degrees from the University of Washington, Liberty Baptist Theological Seminary, and Emerson Theological Institute. He was baptized Catholic, an ordained evangelical Christian pastor at two Seattle mega-churches, a confirmed Episcopalian, an affiliated, licensed minister with the Centers for Spiritual Living, and now the Minister at Unity Center for Spiritual Growth in Couer d'Alene, Idaho. He has a Certificate in Psychedelic Assisted Therapy from Naropa University, trained in Hakomi Mindful Somatic Psychology, and is a certified Coach. He is currently a student in The Living School and the Seminary of the Wild. He considers himself a spiritual explorer, guide, and companion. He believes your way is The Way.

CYNTHIA LINDENMEYER

Reverend Dr. Cynthia Ramirez Lindenmeyer is the Founder of the Sacred Activism Community and serves as Chaplain and Director of Student Wellness for the American Public University System. A graduate of the United States Military Academy at West Point, Duke Divinity School, and Princeton Theological Seminary, she integrates spirituality, psychology, and mystical consciousness in her work. Through extensive experiences with psilocybin and other plant medicines across South America, and as a graduate of the Synthesis Institute's Psychedelic Practitioner Core Training Program, Cynthia brings a depth of metaphysical understanding to her ministry as an ordained minister for Center for Spiritual Living. Her vision centers on awakening humanity to its inherent divinity and spiritual wholeness.

BRYAN DAVID MCCARTHY

Dr. Bryan McCarthy, D.Phil. is a philosophy professor at the University of Pittsburgh, Greensburg. His work investigates how psychedelic drugs might facilitate Christian spirituality. He recently authored "Christianity and Psychedelic Medicine: A Pastoral Approach" and co-authored "Psychedelic Christianity: From evangelical hippies and Roman Catholic intellectuals in the sixties to clergy in a Johns Hopkins clinical trial." Dr. McCarthy currently co-leads a qualitative study of psychedelic experiences with Christian elements (@PittPsyX and psyx.pitt.edu). He is a practicing Roman Catholic.

JIMMY MARSH

Jimmy is a psychotherapist, ordained elder in the United Methodist Church, and co-founder of A Wider Table, an inter-spiritual expression of The Church of the Saviour in Washington DC. He has worked with children, youth, young adults, and families for over 35 years as mentor, spiritual companion, and psychotherapist. He provides guidance and accountability to help young people realize their unique potential. He partners with Faith and Money Network, a non-profit that helps people of faith make that sacred connection. Jimmy is certified through the California Institute of Integral Studies in Psychedelic Therapies and Research, and facilitates "Christic" (Christian Mystic) psychedelic retreats in legal settings.

JONATHAN MYERS

Rev. Jonathan Myers is an Episcopal priest, spiritual director, and artist currently living and serving in Spokane, WA. Having spent years in the evangelical world he migrated to the Pacific Northwest and found a home in the Episcopal Church. With his background he started down an entrepreneurial path of planting churches and intentional communities, with particular attention on people leaving religious trauma and damaging theology. He now serves as the Rector of St. Stephen's Episcopal Church and offers Spiritual Direction specifically for church planters and redevelopers. He is also launching a new practice, co-founding Inner Sky Pilgrimage, which is a year round formation experience through the practice of pilgrimage. As an artist, his abstract work focuses on drawing the eye to the contemplative gaze through color, texture, and negative space.

RUBEN NUÑO

Ruben Nuño serves as Pastor of Church of the Living Hope in East Harlem and as Director of the Ecumenical Outreach Program at Fifth Avenue Presbyterian Church, a collaborative homeless outreach initiative with St. Thomas Episcopal Church and St. Patrick's Cathedral. For more than 20 years, he has led faith-based organizations providing humanitarian assistance in West Africa, Marseille (France), Honduras, and Little Tokyo in Downtown Los Angeles. Since 2018, along with his wife Meghann and 5 children, his ministry in East Harlem has continued the Church of Living Hope's historic advocacy for fair housing policies, empowering immigrant communities, providing youth mentorship, and creating meaningful outreach opportunities for volunteers.

BETSY OUELLETTE-ZIERDEN

Rev. Betsy Ouellette-Zierden, MDiv is a retired United Methodist clergywoman, spiritual director, and writer exploring the intersections of Christian faith, mystical experience, and the emerging psychedelic renaissance. Through her project Christ on the Psychedelic Highway, she invites readers into honest, healing conversations about God's presence in all creation and the surprising ways grace continues to reveal itself in modern spiritual life.

JAN OWEN, M.A., LPC

Jan Owen is an ordained Baptist minister and Licensed Professional Counselor in Alabama where she owns Back Porch Counseling, specializing in grief, trauma, and spiritual issues. She spent 15 years serving as Pastor of Worship Arts and founded the Give Worship Project, providing free educational opportunities for church leaders in under-resourced countries. Jan holds certification in Death and Grief Studies and is currently training in Psychedelic Assisted Therapy with Integrative Psychiatry Institute. Her interest in psychedelics began when she participated in a life-changing journey to help process grief from multiple losses. She is passionate about the potential of psychedelics to help individuals connect with the Creator and find deep healing.

HUNT PRIEST

Hunt Priest served The Episcopal Church as a priest for 20 years. In 2016, he was a fortunate participant in the Johns Hopkins/NYU Psilocybin Study for Religious Professionals. His encounters with psilocybin opened him to the healing and consciousness-raising power of sacred plants and fungi and their connection to his own Christian practice and ministry. The epiphanies forever changed the trajectory of his work. In April 2021 Hunt resigned his position as rector of an Episcopal church in Savannah, Georgia to found Ligare, which works to bridge the knowledge gap between psychedelic research and religious and spiritual communities. In his vocation, he works to put the healing power of the sacred plants in the toolkits of all who are healers of bodies, minds, and souls.

BRIAN RAJCOK

The Rev. Dr. Brian Rajcok is an ordained Lutheran pastor in the Evangelical Lutheran Church in America (ELCA). He serves as senior pastor at St. Matthew Lutheran Church in Avon, CT. He studied theology at Valparaiso University, earned his MDiv at Luther Seminary, and completed his PhD in pastoral counseling at Neumann University where he wrote his doctoral dissertation on spiritually significant psychedelic experiences. He is also a graduate of the California Institute of Integral Studies' Center for Psychedelic Therapies and Research certificate program. Brian is passionate about the study of consciousness, world religions, nature spirituality, and the relationship between science and spirituality, particularly the relationship between contemplative prayer, mysticism, and psychedelic experience. An important part of his spiritual journey is the Christian contemplative practice of centering prayer. He views both psychedelics and contemplative practices as tools for deepening one's relationship with God and cultivating spiritual growth and transformation.

FR GEOFFREY READY

The Very Reverend Dr Geoffrey Ready is the director of Orthodox Christian Studies at Trinity College within the University of Toronto, Canada, where he teaches liturgical theology, pastoral studies, and both Old and New Testament. Fr Geoffrey received his doctorate in liturgical theology focusing on enacted narrative as the formative element of Christian liturgy. His research interests include the narrative and ritual shape of the spiritual journey of transformation — life, death, and resurrection — galvanized by mystical experience, prompted through ancient spiritual practices including the careful use of entheogens. Fr Geoffrey also serves as rector of Holy Myrrhbearers Orthodox Mission, an English language church that worships at Trinity College.

BRENT A. REYNOLDS

Rev. Brent Reynolds is a spiritually oriented traveler and contemplation-led learner with a deep interest in and practice of mindfulness, ecstatic dance, and journey-work. A graduate of the University of Chicago Divinity School, he still struggles on the road between the head and heart, yet remains deeply grateful to be in relationship with people who carry each other with love, grace, dignity, and compassion.

ANDREA SMITH

The Rev. Dr. Andrea Smith is a United Methodist pastor, missional strategist, and community innovator. She is the Lead Pastor of West Church LKN and the Executive Director of Missional Strategy for Level Up Together, a nonprofit dedicated to practical compassion, social enterprise, and community partnerships. Andrea is the creator of SOUL Creations, a mission-driven artisan business, and leads large-scale initiatives such as the Back to School Bash. She is a graduate of Appalachian State University and Wesley Theological

Seminary and is deeply shaped by contemplative Christian practice, integrating wisdom from modern psychology, organizational leadership, and everyday spiritual experience. Her work centers on helping people encounter a faith that is honest, accessible, and grounded in the real needs of the world.

TIMOTHY TUTT

Rev. Dr. Timothy Tutt is a United Church of Christ clergyperson who is currently developing an aquaponics farm in an affordable housing apartment building in the Adams Morgan neighborhood where he lives in Washington DC. Tim is a dad, a native Texan, an avid runner, and is working on a book about the theology of Dolly Parton's music. He is a fan of an intriguing poem, a well-executed double play, and spinach enchiladas.

B. JEFFREY VIDT, MAT, MAR, RP

Jeff Vidt is a spiritual care practitioner and registered psychotherapist at CHEO, a pediatric trauma hospital in Eastern Ontario, Canada. His work is grounded in a gentle, presence-based approach that honours meaning, connection, and the sacred dimensions of grief and suffering.

Jeff was also a participant in the Religious Leaders Study using psilocybin at Johns Hopkins, an experience that deepened his commitment to professional spiritual care in psychedelic therapies. He has served on the Board for the Canadian Association for Spiritual Care and the Multidisciplinary Association for Psychedelic Studies (MAPS) Canada. He currently lives in Ottawa with his wife and two sons.

ROGER WOLSEY

Roger Wolsey is a United Methodist minister and certified spiritual director who brings over 29 years of pastoral experience to his work integrating contemplative practice with contemporary spirituality. He is the author of *Kissing Fish: Christianity for People Who Don't Like Christianity* and *Discovering Fire: Spiritual Practices That Transform Lives*, and serves on the Board of Directors for The Center for Progressive Christianity (ProgressiveChristianity.org). Roger's spiritual journey has been shaped by diverse practices including centering prayer, sacred plant medicine work, and various healing modalities. He has particular gifts in helping people integrate transformative spiritual experiences. A regular contributor to Progressing Spirit and frequent speaker at progressive Christian festivals, Roger is passionate about social justice and creating inclusive spiritual communities. Originally from Minnesota, he now lives in his hometown where he continues his work as a spiritual director, writer, and guide for those navigating life's mysteries.

PAUL INDORF

Raised in the Missouri Lutheran tradition, Paul was drawn to liberal Quakerism in the early 2000s, where he became "convinced" of the truth that there is That of God in each of us—and in all things—and that we can encounter the Divine directly. His subsequent entheogenic experiences with plant medicines and training in indigenous and ancient spiritual practices have deepened this conviction, transforming belief into lived experience. Paul has served on the boards of the Friends Committee on National Legislation and William Penn House, and he currently serves on the boards of the Friends Collaborative on Spirit and Psyche and the Friends Conference on Religion and Psychology. He is also a student in the first cohort of the Sacred Medicine Practitioner Training Program at the Sanctuary for Sacred Union in Boulder, Colorado.

ABOUT MATT ZEMON

 Matt Zemon is a thought leader at the intersection of psychedelics, science, and spiritual experience. After his own profound mushroom experience transformed him from skeptic to seeker, he has been blending academic rigor with compassionate advocacy to promote safer, intentional, and transformative psychedelic use.

Matt is the best-selling author of The Beginner's Guide to Psychedelics, The Veteran's Guide to Psychedelics, Psychedelics for Everyone, and Beyond the Trip: A Journal for Psychedelic Preparation and Integration. He holds a Doctorate of Ministry from Pacific School of Religion and a Master's degree in Psychology and Neuroscience of Mental Health from King's College London.

Through his writing, teaching, and collaboration with medical and spiritual communities, Matt bridges ancient wisdom and modern science to help individuals navigate these profound experiences with clarity and purpose. His work empowers spiritual seekers on the path of personal growth to engage with psychedelics with care, integrity, and respect. www.mattzemon.com

www.ingramcontent.com/pod-product-compliance
Lightning Source LLC
Chambersburg PA
CBHW021213130626
46554CB00004B/1208